How

to

Read Faster

and

Remember

More

Morris N. Young, M. D.

and Chesley V. Young

PARKER PUBLISHING CO., INC.
WEST NYACK, N.Y.

How

to

Read Faster

and

Remember

More

How to Read Faster and Remember More
   by Morris N. Young, M.D., and Chesley V. Young
© 1965 by Parker Publishing Co., Inc.
West Nyack, N. Y.

Library of Congress Card Catalog Number: 65-23060

Printed in the United States of America
43072 B&P

How this book will help you read faster and remember more of everything you've read

Of course you would like to read faster and remember more. The only problem is, it sounds impossible. Each process seemingly would counteract the other, yet such need not be the case.

In the vast majority of reading pursuits, you *can* read faster and at the same time remember more. This book tells *why*. With brief, pointed examples, it stresses how *reading* and *remembering are as one*.

Each is simply a phase of an overall skill or ability. You must have a memory to read, so reading expands that memory. With that key in mind, you are already started on the path toward reading to remember.

By combining the factors of interest, attention and repetition, you will build the power of association that links reading with remembering.

The next step is to apply that dual power. This book tells you *how* the twin factors of reading and remembering may be expanded and developed to a degree that may seem fanciful, yet at the same time will be replete with practical value.

Every related facet of learning, every literary need, every form of daily routine—from a casual memo to a technical treatise

—can be sped and retained more effectively through the blending of reading and remembering into a unified force.

Proper application of these combined techniques to material at hand will pave the way to pyramiding profitable results:

1. You will become fully aware of how to read with speed, confidence and security.

2. You will be guided in skillfully choosing your reading material during the preliminary stages, thus saving time by shelving any that is unimportant and concentrating on whatever is more valuable or essential.

3. Reading without tiring too soon will be made possible through adherence to proper reading conditions which also engender increased retention.

4. You will learn to turn the primitive reading habit of vocalization into the swift, expansive art of visualization.

5. You will learn to develop a knack of sustaining or renewing interest during long reading sessions.

6. You will learn how to go through business correspondence and routine material faster, and remember more of the details that you need in them.

7. Special emergency devices for rapidly memorizing difficult material are made available for your use.

8. You will learn ways of acquiring technical and self-help material with increased speed and assurance.

9. You will be shown how to condense and digest articles on your own, weeding while you read, thereby saving time and eliminating extraneous material.

10. You will find that you can keep better informed, gathering important facts from newspapers in less time than many readers take to go through inconsequential articles.

11. You can turn spare time reading to full use by applying the same efficient measures used in more important reading.

12. You will gain more enjoyment from leisure reading, handling it more smoothly and easily.

13. Speeches, poetry, quotations, can be memorized in a fraction of the time usually taken, and can be retained impressively longer.

14. With mastery of reading and its methods, you will be well on your way toward improving your own status, in matters of leadership, authority, knowledge and dependability.

Table

of

contents

How

to

Read Faster

and

Remember

More

How

more effective

reading

can

I   ## enrich

your life

Why You Must See Reading
and Remembering as One

Reading and remembering are closely interwoven: without memory, you can not read at all. To recognize a word, you must either remember it from somewhere, or be able to identify it by its structure. To read rapidly, recognition must be spontaneous, and newly acquired words must be remembered for future use.

This double process is becoming more and more important, now that the current literary explosion has reached almost fantastic proportions. The demands of informative and technical subjects have also added to the need for faster reading, if only to find time for other things.

Many avid readers complain that they are unable to remember what they read. They blame it on "poor memory" of all things, completely overlooking how closely reading and remembering are related. So before putting yourself in the "poor memory" bracket, read and weigh the following paragraph:

> If you were asked to remember one hundred items or ideas so thoroughly that you could recognize any of them instantly on sight, you might regard it as a difficult or, perhaps, impossible task. Actually, however, it is quite simple, something indeed that is a familiar part of everyday life. All such impressions can be expressed in words

which are the result of various letter combinations, each with its own significance. Therefore, by merely going back through this paragraph and counting the words composing its four sentences—with due allowance, of course, for duplications—you will find that you have utilized your power of memory in the prompt identification of more than one hundred distinctive thoughts, each represented by an individual word.

This, in a sense, puts you in the same category as the memory expert who can call off a hundred objects in regular rotation or remember the names of persons and match them by looking at their faces. The chief difference is in the application, for the same basic elements are involved.

In reading, you go through a process so close to memorizing that the two are equivalent, if not identical. By teaming reading techniques with memory methods, you can use each to advance the other, with the result that you will remember what you read more vividly and more effectively.

There are certain factors that are vital both to memory and reading. These include

1. Interest.
2. Attention.
3. Repetition.

Each of these three plays a varying part, according to the subject demanding memorization or the type of reading involved.

How To Achieve Interest
In Everything You Read

While some interest is essential in every case, the necessity for it is more important whenever the mind is turned into a difficult channel. A person must be sufficiently interested in a subject to give it the amount of thought required to learn more about it.

Interest, therefore, may be measured in terms of intensity.

A person anxious to become an actor will devote time to memorizing lines, because this is necessary in order to further that interest. Similarly, anyone who wants to play football realizes that he must study plays and memorize signals. A would-be politician recognizes the need for remembering people by their names and faces in order to get their votes.

The interest factor applies just as strongly to reading, but with a deceptive twist. Interest in certain types of reading can cause a person to neglect others, even reading which is supplementary to the main type. Some readers will completely ignore anything that does not interest them.

Actually, it is a bad reading habit to wade through material mechanically, but some balance is necessary between "light" and "heavy" reading. The interest factor has important bearing and should be applied accordingly. The main point is that reading, like memorizing, is a means to an end, rather than a purpose in itself.

This holds true even with this book, with its aim of HOW TO READ FASTER AND REMEMBER MORE. The real interest is in *acquiring* facts more rapidly and *retaining* more of them. Reading and memorization are simply processes used to attain this dual goal.

However, the means itself must be developed to achieve the end. If anything is worth reading and remembering, some step must be taken to stimulate interest, when it is lax. The simplest way is to extend the "picture book" method, used to develop progressive interest in reading.

This time-tested system begins with alphabet blocks running from "A" for *Antelope* to "Z" for *Zebra*. It goes on to books with action pictures, then to illustrated editions, and *finally* to a single illustration in the form of a book jacket. This picture alone can be enough to interest a reader in the entire text.

How "Making Pictures" Sustains Interest

To give yourself an interest in a tough but necessary reading assignment, try to visualize it as you would the cover of a book. To sustain that interest, picture it as you proceed. Simulate interest in order to stimulate it. Think back to some picture that aroused your interest in connection with an article or book and try to go it one better with the subject at hand. Such picturization links reading with remembering, thereby strengthening the interest factor.

Here is a classic example of this: During his college days, Robert Benchley, the famous humorist, was asked to write a report on the activities of the Northwest Fisheries Commission, treating it from a new and interesting viewpoint. While other students tangled with statistics, economics and political problems, Benchley found just the slant he wanted. He wrote his report from the standpoint of a fish. Nobody ever forgot that one.

How To Maintain
Your Attention While Reading

No matter how great interest in a subject may be, it is useless unless followed by attention. A person interested in chemistry, for example, will get nowhere unless he is willing to learn chemical formulas or undertake chemical experiments.

In this era of multiple activities, we frequently encounter "experts" whose range of knowledge consists of wishful thinking which deflates itself before reaching a substantial stage. This applies both to reading and remembering. Each has its pitfalls where attention is concerned, but in the field of reading, they are apt to prove more deadly.

Many people will blame their "poor memory" for their inability to remember things. In so doing, they show an interest in improvement and are willing to accept suggestions. But few will admit that they are bad readers. In fact, the very worst readers often class themselves among the best.

Lack of attention is frequently the real fault. A person who goes in for cooking and fails to get results, will generally admit that he did not study the recipe properly. An amateur photographer who takes poor pictures will agree that he should first learn how to use a camera. This is not so with ordinary reading. People regard the ability to read as something inborn and are unwilling to concede that their ability could be improved.

If you ask a person about something he has "read" and he is unable to reel it off, he will fall back on the "poor memory" argument and say that he has "forgotten" it, or that something he read later crowded it from his mind.

Actually, he didn't remember it because he didn't read it properly.

However, if you tell him that, he won't believe it.

He will say, "Why, I've been reading since I was in first grade and now you are telling me I don't know how!"

Of course, he does know how; that is, how to read the way he did in first grade!

Perhaps he still reads now as he did then, without showing any great improvement.

Or has he improved?

Using Attention Getters
to Sustain Interest

The answer can lie in his development of attention. Most of his reading will be beyond the interest stage. But will he stay with it? Can he sustain that interest through attention? In simple reading, there are many "attention getters." You have just run through a series of them, consisting of short sentences with quotations, exclamations and finally a question mark. All those sentences were set in individual paragraphs, so they would be sure to capture your attention.

That is the formula used in basic reading and it is also a trick of editors and other writers, when they are anxious to drive home a "message." But it becomes stilted and monotonous when applied to narrative, descriptive and other forms of writing that demand more elaboration. It is then up to the reader to maintain his own attention. To do this, he must gain facility in breaking down sentences, following changes of thought and increasing his reading comprehension.

Attention has its physical as well as its mental side. Proper light is essential and the eyes should be checked periodically by a physician, so that correcting lenses can be worn as required. Quiet and comfort are important factors, as they provide the necessary concentration and exclude distractions.

At the same time, it is important to remain alert. Once attention lags, or drifts into a dreamy state, it is time for a break and a new start. This is true both in reading and remembering, for the two are firmly intertwined. Any lag of attention will evidence itself through lack of recollection, so the way to check it is through brief, regular pauses to make sure you have absorbed what you just read.

In fiction as well as in some forms of factual reading, chapters provide the customary breaks needed for such reveiw, while technical books frequently have subheads that are helpful. Highly important are the questions that often appear at the end of a chapter, for these are directly linked with the third factor in reading to remember, namely: REPETITION.

Using Repetition
to Nail Down Facts

There is a humorous anecdote about a man who was isolated in a lumber camp by a flood and was unable to leave for a month or so. All he could find to read was an odd volume of an encyclopedia that someone had forgotten to take along. So he read it, day after day.

In the years that followed, people who met the man were astounded by his vast and detailed knowledge on any subject that happened to begin with the letters M or N.

This, of course, is a whimsical case; but years ago, people did read works of their favorite authors over and over, until they could recite passages from memory. What is more, they gained a fuller understanding, up to a certain point, through such repetition. Today, the re-reading of entire poems or speeches has proved a better way of memorization, than reading them in piecemeal fashion.

As applied to general reading, where a person desires to remember the substance of material read only once, repetition asserts itself in a most subtle way. Through frequent reading, in which the reader becomes faster and more efficient, a familiarity is gained with words and phrases that makes the material itself more mentally digestible and therefore better remembered.

Proof of this is found in many ways, from the reading of a newspaper to highly technical data, dependent of course, upon the individual reader. The whole pattern of the average news story is geared to the taste of the so-called "constant reader" who revels in each day's edition and occasionally writes in opinions to the editor.

Similarly, the most complex writing in scientific fields is usually understandable at sight to persons familiar with its forms. In both cases—news reader and technician alike—two points are particularly noteworthy: The *speed* with which the material is absorbed and the *amount* of it that the individual retains in mind. While someone else would be struggling even to grasp the brisk lingo of the news columnist or the nomenclature of the technical writer, persons familiar with such material not only *read* it but *remember* it .

Here, of course, we have INTEREST plus ATTENTION; however, it is the third factor, Repetition, that leads to increased efficiency. It is not entirely a case of reading exactly the same thing over and over; it is reading the same *type* of thing repeatedly. Catchwords, phrases, technical terms, formulas may appear time and again in new or different connections; but they link with old memories and are recognizable on sight.

Now, between these extremes of the avid news reader and the knowledgeable technician, the same principles of reading and re-

membering can be applied to many other fields. Arouse your
interest, apply your attention and read enough of a subject to reach
the point where repetition plays its part. From then on, you will
begin to read faster and remember more.

Note than these reading speeds will vary, as will the amount
remembered, due both to the type of material and individual
familiarity with it; but the more the reading and the broader its
scope, the greater the interchange of ideas from subject to subject
and the higher the overall efficiency.

Mastering the Key to Memory: Association

The three vital factors, INTEREST, ATTENTION and REPETI-
TION, lead to ASSOCIATION, which is the great key to memory. In
fact, memorization itself has been defined as a series of associations,
stimulated individually or collectively by the components of interest, attention and repetition.

Give the mind any idea and it will immediately link up others,
either in chains or clusters. The stronger these links, or the greater
their number, the better the initial idea will be remembered. What
is more, you do not have to be conscious of these links. Such
associations are constantly at work in the mind, so that a thought
may seem to jump abruptly from one idea to another quite far
removed; yet an analysis will show that there were many links,
real or *suggested,* in between.

Thus, a person might form a logical link of the words, *school,
bus, highway, bridge, brook, river, ocean, boat, whistle.* Later,
the same person might think of *school* and link it immediately with
whistle; then wonder why he thought of a school with a whistle
instead of a bell!

Erasure of the in-between links is, of course, responsible. That
is why persons have childhood recollections of odd things that go
together without rational connection. For a similar reason, old

reading habits and rules of spelling may crop up unexpectedly. They were linked to something that impressed the youthful mind; but later, the reading process became smoother and somewhat automatic.

Using Visualization to Read More Effectively

In every association there is usually more than a linkage of mere ideas. A picture may be formed, an action visualized, a sensation experienced, an auditory impression gained, culminating in the spoken word. Often, these are combined into one instantaneous association.

With the written word "boat," you might instantly *picture* a boat, then *visualize* it moving through the water, *experience* the sensation of being on the boat, gain the *auditory* impression of the motor or the surge of water; and immediately sum up all of these by apparently *hearing* the spoken word BOAT.

Often, the association is so strong that a person will actually say the word aloud. This is a common process with unfamiliar words, an instinctive effort to fix them in the memory through repetition. This in turn, can be responsible for one of the worst of reading habits, "vocalization," which will be dealt with in a later chapter.

Reading is slowed and therefore hindered through vocalization, or the reading of words half-aloud. But if it serves as a memory peg for unfamiliar words, how can a reader get along without it?

Very simply. It is done by discarding *vocalization* in favor of *visualization*. Instead of slowing things by *saying* the word, you *picture* it as you see it on the printed page, all in one glance. From this, you gradually develop a very remarkable ability, which you may not realize; and one that has been overlooked in many reading surveys.

Don't Vocalize—Visualize

Going back to our cluster of associations surrounding the word "boat," there is one which was not listed, yet which with many people is the keynote. They do not just *hear* the word "boat" amid the surge of varied impressions; they *see* it in printed or written form.

The Ancients treated writing as a picturization, in which symbols gradually supplanted actual images. The formation of the alphabet simply introduced a new way of making pictures to represent things. Such words as BOAT or BIRD or GRASS are just as distinctive and definitive as a quick sketch or drawing would be.

Think of any simple word, shut your eyes and you will find that the word itself begins to form. As the associations are stimulated, the word may fade; but there are instances where it may become dominant.

If someone mentions a bowl of "crackers and soup," the appetizing picture of a bowl of steaming soup may crowd out other impressions. You may see crackers floating in it and the result may be a sensation of taste or hunger. The words CRACKERS and SOUP may be obliterated at the very start.

In contrast, if a person speaks of a bowl of "curds and whey," your impression is apt to resolve itself into those two words. You may visualize a bowl filled with some indefinable substance, but CURDS and WHEY will predominate. If you worry enough about them, you will look them up in the dictionary and you won't forget how to spell them until you find out what they are, provided of course, that you don't already know.

In recalling familiar objects, people often think of an object first; then the word that describes it. With unfamiliar objects the word may be the only clue by which you can later identify it. In either case, the law of association works interchangeably.

Sometimes, when doodling with paper and pencil, a person may write a name or word that he wants to remember, just as he might repeat it aloud. Here, again, association is the motivating factor and it fits with the general guideline that every reader should remember:

Don't vocalize. VISUALIZE *

Reading, therefore, becomes a language in itself, requiring translation from the spoken to the written word and vice versa. As printed words take on an individuality of their own, word study paves the way to more effective reading and to clearer understanding.

How More Effective Reading
Can Enrich Your Life

They used to say, "There is no royal road to learning." But today there is. That royal road is through reading, which in the past few decades has increased from ten to a hundred times over. Facts are now presented in more palatable and efficient form, aimed at specific types of readers. In the old days, you had to understand a subject the way the writer told it; today, the writer tells it so you can understand it.

Hence, reading leads directly to learning, through absorption and memorizing of facts and logic patterns. The greater the scope of your reading, the greater the interplay of facts and their evaluation. Learning, in its turn, increases reading facility, because the common factor, memory, works two ways.

Along with general learning, reading can be directed to specific purposes, which come under the following heads:

READING TO GET AHEAD

Today, this is a prime requisite in reading, the great reason why everyone must read faster and remember more. The world is moving faster and a sure way to get ahead is to accept its tempo. This does not mean that life has become a mad whirl; far from it.

---

* See Chapter IV for exceptions.

What it does mean is that today, a man may go more places, meet more people and undergo more new experiences in a year than his grandfather did in an entire lifetime. In those days, reading was necessary to get ahead; and that rule still stands. There was a lot more time then for reading up on things, just as it took a longer time for those things to materialize.

The jobs of tomorrow go to the men who have learned them today. Only through reading can you follow the current trends.

READING TO KEEP UP

With many people, simply keeping up is as important as getting ahead is to others. In every field, from politics to astrophysics, changes are occuring at a kaleidoscopic pace. No one can afford to ignore the world about him, or he won't know what the world is all about.

READING FOR RECREATION

With all the emphasis on more reading, it would seem that the recreational side would suffer. Actually, the only one who suffers is the reader who ignores his recreational reading. In its way, reading has become so important a part of every person's life that reading, in itself, must be balanced.

According to a long quoted proverb, no one's life should be "all work and no play." That applied chiefly to physical effort, thought it goes for the mental and the intellectual as well. Persons connected with the literary field have recognized that, this long while. The man who delves heavily into facts finds recreation in reading fiction. Heavy scientific reading can be lightened by reading up on sports and hobbies.

Balance your reading as you would your diet. It will increase your scope, broaden your approach and improve your reading ability.

READING FOR OCCUPATIONAL KNOWLEDGE

This, of course, is a "must" in reading and here the reader should seek new channels along with supplementary forms of reading. There is nothing that makes a subject so boring as staying too close to it. Occupational readers often slow themselves through their own limitations.

In this form of reading, every phase of the occupation should be considered. News items referring to a business, articles in trade journals, all are as important as the standard reference books, sometimes more so, as they present angles of their own. Don't be a plodder in occupational reading. Here, as much as anywhere, the rules for reading faster and remembering more should be studied and applied in full.

READING FOR RESEARCH PURPOSES

As with occupational reading, this type of reading should be broadened and varied. Many persons regard research as culling general facts from similar sources and pooling them into a single hodge-podge. That is why research has been humorously defined as "Taking material from books that nobody ever reads and putting it into books that nobody ever will read."

In reading for research, a good plan is to delve into sources well removed from the basic subject, thus getting outside opinions and viewpoints, the very thing that you, as a research reader, are hoping to develop. Again, reading faster and remembering more are practical ways to link the associations gained.

READING TO ACQUIRE FACTS

This is a specialized form of reading that should be carefully planned. Acquisition of facts is useless unless they are retained and classified, so here, memory methods are of paramount importance. Such reading and remembering will be discussed in detail in a later chapter.

READING FOR SELF-DEVELOPMENT

Today, this is perhaps the most important type of reading. It covers a great variety of subjects, including the types of reading already listed. One point should be stressed here: namely, that reading in itself is a form of self-development.

In this field, therefore, two things can be accomplished simultaneously. It is possible to acquire facts, keep up with modern trends, or whatever else you wish; and at the same time increase your ability in that direction.

Proper application to the types of reading previously given, progressive efforts to improve and speed your reading in such fields, is an automatic step to self-development.

In summary all of the reading purposes listed require varied reading speeds, gauged in terms of comprehension, or the ability to grasp and understand what has been read. The prime purpose in faster reading is not just to save time, however desirable that may be. It is to improve comprehension, by increased reading efficiency.

Tests have shown that plodding reading, like hesitating spoken sentences, is less coherent than a smooth, well-timed process. The faster the reading, the fuller the grasp of individual phrases and greater the comprehension, up to a certain point.

A simple analogy is found in expert typing records which have reached a speed of 150 words a minute, with an error of less than one per cent. Compare this with the clumsy, two-finger method which is slow and filled with mistakes and you have the answer where reading is concerned.

More reading is possible through faster reading which speeds the memory processes. Increased familiarity with words improves facility in reading them. The faster you read, the more you will remember; and the more you remember, the faster you can read.

Reading, however, must first be geared to remembering more important things. Extra speed becomes possible when memorization is not needed, as with recreational reading. But that speed-up will help extend the memory process, with the final result in synchronization of reading and remembering, which can reach its full efficiency through careful selection of material and use of the methods that follow.

Maximizing results with better reading conditions

II

This chapter tells how modern reading has become more complex than reading used to be. As with driving a car, or exercising any other advanced skill, speed and concentration are essential. Surroundings and other conditions are considered in relationship to reading and remembering.

Importance of lighting, both natural and artificial, is stressed in this chapter. The position of the book, the avoidance of glare, the cultivation of good reading habits are given attention in some detail. The physical phases of reading, and their bearing on the mental processes of remembering are correlated here.

Efficiency of reading ability can be a key to physical fitness. Along with this, the utility of exercise and rest periods as aids to memorization are discussed. Good reading and good health are teamed up as vital factors in reading to remember.

We have stressed that reading is a special skill and that its acquisition, with the added purpose of remembering what you read, should be regarded as a definite project capable of continued improvement.

Modern reading has gone so far beyond old-fashioned concepts and has become so vital a factor in the lives of so many people, that it is no longer comparable simply to walking, swimming, or other skills that are largely instinctive. In keeping with today's tempo, reading has become an activity which in its complexity is much like driving a car.

How Modern Reading Can Be
Compared to Driving

Let us pursue that analogy further. Suppose a man tried to read a newspaper while driving a car along a highway at 50 miles an hour. It seems ridiculous to think that he could absorb dozens of headlines, editorials, three or four advertising pages and a comic section under such circumstances. Yet, that is not at all odd.

Many drivers do so regularly, but not with small print. Instead, they do distant reading. That includes billboards with their ads, announcements and jokes. Also gasoline service stations, with their brand names, discounts on tires, oil changes, premium offers. It includes data on motels, restaurants, and places to visit. There are also many road signs and highway markers that are required reading in this long-range literary assortment. Count up the wordage and the total will surprise you.

Through the years, they have been on the increase, implying that as people have learned to drive faster, they have learned to read faster, too. This is a far cry from the horse-and-buggy days when there were only crossroad guide posts that people stopped to study at leisure. With automobiles, road signs were enlarged and some were painted like pages of big books, telling about historic sights. But traffic became too heavy for motorists to slow down and read those.

New signs sprang up, some with disconnected jingles, a sign for each line, so that drivers could pick them up like phrase reading. There were protests against highway billboards, but not because they distracted the driver. The fault was, they spoiled the scenery! Just about nobody cared how far a driver's eyes and mind wandered in those days. But with superhighways and turnpikes, the law began to limit signs to those that had to do with driving, as speed limits, turnpike exits, miles to food and fuel, toll gates and the like.

Exactly as with driving, two things are essential in today's reading: Speed and concentration. Instead of the 20 m.p.h. speed on many country roads, we have the 70 m.p.h. speed allowable on some turnpikes. During the years, reading speed standards have increased proportionately. People begin to read fast, just as they drive fast, and learn to think fast.

Obviously, the man who drives at 70 has to be a lot better driver than one who can only hit 20. Today, some freeways have rules compelling drivers to keep going over 40, or be fined for obstructing traffic. So don't obstruct your reading time and penalize yourself by reading too slowly, particularly when it is a recognized fact that speedier reading is not only the vogue but actually can be more efficient.

When you drive, you concentrate on one purpose, but with it, you include reading road signs or noting whatever factors are relevant to the task in hand. In reading, you do the same thing. You allow for interruptions or outside disturbances, if only to keep them under proper control. In fact, you must be aware of your surroundings or you may lapse into an indifference that will defeat your main aim.

At this point, we are thinking chiefly in terms of physical conditions as applied to reading, which is all the more reason why the analogy with driving is so apt.

How Limited Physical Comfort
Adds to Reading Skill

In driving, you would make sure that the car was in running order, and the gas tank filled. You would see that the seat was properly adjusted, that you had proper sunglasses handy if the day proved too bright for you, and that your headlights were in order for night driving. You would want a clean windshield and an unobstructed rear view mirror.

All these help you drive better. You can't let yourself go to sleep when you drive, so you can't afford to be fatigued when you start. You can't take a route that is too scenic, or you might not reach your destination soon enough. Remember that if you become hungry, you will be wasting time looking for restaurant signs and stopping to eat. If there are to be other people in the car, it's a good plan to make sure they aren't or don't become back seat drivers!

Similar factors apply to reading. It may seem nice to read in a comfortable easy chair at home, all fully relaxed. But is it? Perhaps it is like sitting too far back in the driver's seat, ready to enjoy the scenery, or to read too many road signs, or to go to sleep at the wheel at night. Lazy surroundings can lead to lazy reading, mentally as well as physically. Often, a person may lapse into a slow reading speed just through comfort or indifference.

In the theater, actors speak of having an audience "on the edges of their seats." That means that the show has become so dramatic, so all-absorbing, that members of the audience have forgotten their physical comfort. The same applies to reading, but it is best for you to introduce the "seat edge" principle before you start. Don't try to be too comfortable, any more than you would in driving. Suit the comfort to the project, remembering that your critical job is to keep alert.

How to Avoid
Bad Reading Conditions

While good surroundings are helpful and often essential to serious reading, acceptability may vary greatly depending on the reader and what has to be read. Often, avid readers carry books with them and read them under all sorts of conditions. Ideal surroundings are not always obtainable to suit individual needs. A most practical procedure is to set certain minimum standards and make sure that your reading conditions come up to those. Otherwise, be ready to face up to slowdowns.

• *Proper lighting* is of prime consideration. Without sufficient light, reading is impossible; and sometimes a little too much light makes it worse by encouraging the reader to accept difficult conditions when he would do better not to read at all. Poor light is a cause of eye strain and mental fatigue, which result in inefficient reading methods. With that in mind, it is wise to plan conditions beforehand and more so because if you become deeply engrossed in your reading, those conditions may change without you realizing it.

• *Daylight reading* is, of course, the most natural form, and once was about the only type advisable. That accounts partly for the limited amount of reading prior to the development of modern illumination. School hours were long because reading and studying were virtually synonymous. When you picture young Abe Lincoln at home in a one-room log cabin, scratching out his homework with a slate pencil on the back of a shovel by the light from a log fire, it seems pathetic indeed.

Yet the plight of some modern daylight readers is perhaps equally sad. Commuters read their newspapers on their way to work, only to have the light become a series of blinks, when passing stations or strings of freight cars. That is why many of them turn prudently to crossword puzzles, bridge problems, or comic strips. Those types of literature allow for interruptions.

How and What to Read
While Traveling

Reading by daylight in a bus or car may prove even more troublesome. A plane may provide good daylight reading when you get high above the clouds and into a realm of continuous sunlight. Business men do a great deal of important reading on planes, and less on trains and buses. In these situations, the reading should be of an intermittent type, allowing for more breaks and relaxation. These can then be timed possibly to the forced interruptions of daylight.

Under conditions of train and bus travel, the reader is aware of outside factors and accepts them, just as an automobile driver, while watching the road, reads warning signs and also gathers information from other announcements that he sees along the road-side.

On trains, editors can read and correct manuscripts, students may review assignments and take notes, business men may go over reports and correspondence, all to good avail. Newspaper reading, too, has its place under such conditions, provided it follows a "scanning" pattern while looking for special items and probing them briefly. It is a case of "stop" and "go" just like the warning signs that the car driver heeds before all else.

Why Sustained Reading
Is Difficult

Otherwise, a reader may defeat himself two ways, if he undertakes "sustained" reading under "intermittent" circumstances as described. He wastes time with forced breaks, thereby decreasing his reading and memory efficiency; and he falls into jumpy habits, making it difficult to gain the rhythm so valuable to speed reading.

Persons who force themselves to over-reading on the morning bus or train may find it hardly a tranquilizing way to start the day. If that is your experience, try not to "jump the gun" where the day's reading is concerned. Another test would be to do the same type of reading at the end of the day instead of at the beginning and compare results.

There is another group of readers who find that their zest for news wears off between the morning newspaper and the evening edition, or that chapters of a book read on the way to work were more interesting than those read on the way home. If so, reading conditions may be to blame, perhaps quite as much as the day's fatigue.

How to Use Daylight
When Reading Indoors

At home or in the office, a more or less gradual change of natural light takes place during the day, causing a lack of uniformity that can prove tiring or troublesome during extensive reading. Generally speaking, the less desirable source of daylight comes from windows facing to the east or west; for in one case, it will diminish as the day progresses and in the other, it will increase. Either way, the daylight will not be consistent.

Similarly, when reading outdoors or on a porch, changes in brightness occur, and shadows can lengthen across the pages of a book, producing a variety of effects that hamper reading and force the eyes to greater effort. Indoors, during daylight when a person is reading in a large room with too few windows, a gradual darkening can prove very deceptive to him. Sometimes, you may walk into such a room and find him reading in what seems to be semi-darkness.

This, of course, should be avoided. Don't let gloom creep in upon your reading habits, not if you can help it! But be wary in regard to counter-measures. It would seem that one sure cure would be to do all your reading close by the window in the light of day; but here, the remedy may produce a greater problem. Instead of gloom, you may encounter glare.

When the daylight comes too strongly from one side, it is excessively uneven, so that one page of the book is uncomfortably brighter than the other. If the reader aids the far eye by moving closer to the daylight, the other eye may be more troubled by excessive reflection or glare. Next, in "balancing up" he may point the book squarely into the light, in such a way that both eyes catch the over-brightness or glare.

In choosing a good room for reading, and to take the fullest advantage of daylight, avoid hazards such as flowered or patterned window curtains that will cause the daylight to be blotchy. Colored curtains may create problems, casting light of their own hue. In your home or apartment, you can often establish more satisfactory conditions, and when elsewhere, you should try to approximate your accustomed reading environment.

Avid readers who carry books everywhere and pore over them at odd moments may find this difficult. Usually, they seem to have a penchant for picking the best available light, though they may be less finicky about other things.

One must surmise then, that because of the fickle nature of daylight, it cannot be depended on as a constantly efficient source of light for extensive reading indoors. However, it can be supplemented with artificial light, to provide useful reading illumination that detracts least from memory intake.

Reading by Artificial Light

It is possible to create almost any lighting condition desired for reading, though too few people give it much thought. Over the years, there have been two problems where such light was concerned: quantity and quality. Even with the advent of electricity, many people still continued to read by light that was too feeble or too flickery. Today, with unlimited power, there has been a tendency to use excessively strong lighting. To offset this, special bulbs that soften the glare have been introduced. Despite this, the emphasis on brightness persists.

When light was limited, there were many reading who preferred "a good light over the left shoulder." A "strong" light from any position in back is practical, provided no shadows are cast on what you are reading, and the matter of side being guided by your personal inclination. How strong a light is subject to experiment, judging by your own reading comfort, and remembering that you can probably do with less. With modern illumination, overhead lights as planned by competent architects or illuminating engineers are usually satisfactory, though bridge or desk lamps may have to be added to suit your needs. The thing most to be avoided is looking into a light shining from in front of your eyes.

How to Position the Book for
Effective, Comfortable Reading

We have mentioned that the book should be held so that the light comes evenly upon its pages, but that it should not be thrust squarely into the light in such a way that the pages themselves can reflect dense brightness or glare. This is especially true with glossy paper, but in any case, when you read, you are continually viewing that uncomfortable background to the type.

Small type is harder to read than average size, and some type styles are more difficult than others. But often, the reader who feels that his eyes are strained and blames it on the kind of type, actually may be troubled only by the glare from the page. Curiously, a somewhat parallel problem arises when you study a photostat negative, where the letters appear as white upon the black background. The printing will be sharp enough, but you will find yourself groping along.

The glare factor represents a well-known hazard in relation to modern lighting. Attempts to overcome it reach out in many directions, as for example the use of special blue-tinted playing cards in bridge tournaments where participants are continually studying glazed white surfaces under strong illumination.

Avoid Glare or Reflection

Not to be overlooked are the glare or reflections which sometimes come from the surface behind the book being read, such as a glass top desk. One solution is to cover this with a dull green blotter, a color which seems to be least troublesome to most users. The subject of backgrounds also introduces the factor of *contrast*. Under the same lighting conditions, the page of a book looks brighter against a dark than against a light background. Extremes of either may prove uncomfortable and more quickly tiring.

To avoid glare from a light that is either too strong or wrongly placed, a reader may instinctively raise the top part of the book to offset it. This often produces the other extreme. There may still be plenty of light, but the reader isn't getting it where he should. As a result, he is reading in relative semi-darkness, frequently without realizing it. The same is true if his body blocks the light. This may force him to shift the book to a bad angle, producing other complications.

How to Sit for Better Reading

Normally, a reader should be seated in an upright position, holding the book at about waist level, and tilted upward at an angle of 45°. He can rest it on one hand, or against a table if need be, though some readers like to hold the book about equally balanced in both hands.

His head should be tilted slightly down, just enough to allow his eyes to turn comfortably downward, looking almost perpendicular to the open book. The overall position should be such that the light falls evenly on the pages.

The distance of the book from the eyes should be about a half arm's length (13 to 16 inches), but this, like the angle at which the book is tilted, may vary with individual readers. Any tendency to draw the book closer to the eyes by doubling the elbows or thrusting it further by extending the arms, should be checked. Either action may be due to poor light, but they are more likely to indicate a need for corrective lenses.

Holding a book upright, or letting it lie flat, are both bad reading habits. Lifting the book, necessitating a back tilt of the head, may be due to bad lighting. But it may also signify the lazy reader who likes to lie on a couch or bed, with his head propped on a pillow while he stares up at the book he is reading.

Letting a book lie flat forces the reader to view the page at too wide a forward angle, which also is detrimental to effective reading. When a book is flat on the table, the reader is apt to hunch forward on his elbows to read it. Another undesirable habit is to lay the book on the floor and sprawl there to read it.

These and all other bizarre reading postures are to be avoided.

They are common with juvenile readers, who tend to gradually outgrow them. But unless such habits are soon discouraged, they result in restlessness that retards both efficient reading and memorization.

Start Using these Good Reading Habits

1. GET IN SHAPE

You must be in shape for reading, just as with any other project that combines mental and physical activity. The term "physical" should not come as a surprise, for it is quite influential in any session of sustained reading and gains in importance as the reading becomes more serious.

Eye movements and the holding of the book require muscular action, and to a more moderate degree, so does the act of sitting up and the turning of each page. As with all physical effort, there are lulls between. These occur at such times as when the reader may rest his eyes or use them in other ways; also when he may close the book or lay it aside, while he stretches his arms and perhaps reevaluates the lighting conditions.

2. KNOW WHEN TO EXERT MORE EFFORT

Actually, up to that point, the reader has been doing physical work which can be likened to that of a man who has been driving a car along a turnpike at an off-hour when traffic is so light that he has merely to keep his hands on the wheel assisted by power steering. Of course, if traffic became heavier, the driver would have to expend more physical effort. So, for that matter, would the reader, under equivalent circumstances.

With serious or specialized reading, he may be taking notes as he goes along. He may pause to consult a dictionary or encyclopedia and may lay his original reading aside in order to check other sources and references. This is specially true when he is reading to remember, and it may apply where comparatively light reading is involved, as looking up data in connection with a historical novel, to learn if the author is adhering to fact.

3. KNOW WHAT TO AVOID AND WHEN

These diversions are like a driver taking a turnoff from the turnpike, stopping for gas, checking the air in his tires, or following a few side roads before coming back to the main highway, perhaps looking at a map in the meantime. Again, the analogy to reading is plain. Both reader and driver must be more mentally alert and physically active in the cases specified. You must be in shape for both reading and driving. Let us consider some salient physical factors normally involved as they directly affect reading.

• *Avoid reading on an "empty stomach."* The gnawing pangs of hunger can assert themselves too readily into your subconscious. The things you read suggest mental pictures that can not be as readily developed if another more compelling image is already present. If your reading brings up thoughts of food, they easily become predominant; otherwise, you may lose interest entirely. You will be like a man starting on a drive intending to get places fast, only to loiter along looking for a hamburger sign.

There are times when you may start reading intending to take a light snack while you go along. Reading while eating is not a recommended practice. Aside from other difficulties, anyone doing so might soon find himself violating the next maxim.

• *Avoid reading directly after a heavy meal.* Here, the tendency is to become mentally sluggish. Even if you start off reading well, the physical effects of a greatly burdened digestive process can act to gradually slow you down. Anyone who has finished a big Thanksgiving dinner recognizes the tendency to lounge around or even go to sleep afterward. The same applies to almost any sizeable meal in corresponding degree. A bowl of soup or a sandwich should not be enough to cramp your reading style, but anything more might.

Between meals or after your last meal of the day are the

times in which to do your best reading and remembering. In keeping with the above discussions, and other practical considerations, the most difficult periods are in the hour before or after times of expected meals.

Next in logical sequence is a self-evident truth that is frequently disregarded.

• *Avoid reading when tired.* When mentally tired, such advice is automatic, as you aren't apt to be in a reading mood. But it also applies to times when you are physically exhausted, though that is when some people try to read because they can't do much else.

Sleep is needed to regain physical as well as mental stamina, so no matter how alert your mind may seem, a tired body will demand rest just as a hungry stomach craves food. Bodily aches will supplant reading urge and soon you will be seeking the comfort that lessens reading efficiency.

Reading in bed will simply provide that much more comfort, quickening the trend toward sleep. Some people like to read in bed. Under those circumstances, they should not hope to continue a sustained reading process at a high level of efficiency. Usually, they will become drowsy, which may be a desirable aim in itself.

How to Set Up Productive Reading Conditions

Proper environment is essential to efficient reading. Quiet is an important factor, as there should be no distractions. This helps to induce a tranquil state of mind, but the reader must also be mentally alert. Conditions like these, though desirable, are not always attainable. As a result, many readers learn in effect to shut out noise and other disturbances, thinking that will accomplish the same end.

• *Don't accept distractions—get rid of them.* Such a notion is a great mistake. At best, it is only a compromise. Persons who can override distractions still would do better without them. Never waste part of your reading efficiency to overcome obstacles that can be eliminated or avoided. The hushed atmosphere of a library or a secluded study is relished as a result of long experience on the part of intelligent readers. Seek such surroundings when you can.

Often, readers learn to disregard some disturbing factor while engaged in a familiar form of reading. A man at a newspaper "copy desk" manages to read right along, despite the clatter of typewriters. People go about reading novels or even studying certain subjects while hearing a musical program on the radio. These sounds have a way of blurring into a mental background or blending with the reading process.

But when the reader tackles unfamiliar material, or finds that special concentration is necessary, those sounds usually assert themselves too strongly. Furthermore, addition of other factors can prove jarring, such as singing along with music. Anything above a certain level of familiarity will infringe upon the reader's concentration. This simply emphasizes the fact that disturbances should be avoided as much as possible. Where they exist, the efficiency of the reading and memory processes is lowered.

When you must fit yourself to some reading environment, it is a good plan to weigh other conditions besides lighting and quiet. Your eyes and ears are not the only sense organs that can be disturbed to the detriment of efficient reading. You should make sure that the room is the right temperature, and can be maintained at such; also that it is well ventilated, and free from smoke, particularly if it bothers your eyes.

• *Know how to relax while reading.* Exercise and rest periods are essential to efficient reading and remembering. During long reading sessions, about every half hour or if you become groggy, it helps to take a "five-minute break" for a stroll, limbering up and clearing any mental cobwebs. At times it is effective to walk about while reading, a policy that some teachers occasionally adopt with their classes. Actors use this method, too, when working up a part, because it simulates action on the stage. The average reader, however, will probably find it more advantageous to rest his eyes and mind while taking his physical exercise.

How Reading and Good Health
Go Hand-in-Hand

One great advantage of reading is that it is a key to how fit you are keeping yourself. Efficiency of body promotes efficiency of mind. When you lose the desire to read, it may be a sign of physical fatigue, or some unsuspected ailment. This often is first noticeable in your inability to remember what you read, showing how closely remembering and reading are interlocked.

You may go through the motions of reading, absorbing words as such, keeping up a spasmodic interest that seems genuine. But when what you read fails to register in your memory, much as spoken words sometimes fail to impress your ear, it may indeed be a sign that you are feeling below par, though you may not realize it.

Your eyes are an important index to your fitness. Sometimes you may think that your eyes are tired from reading because your eyelids are becoming droopy. It may be that your mind is tired and is rebelling against the forced reading process. We all know that people who "just can't keep their eyes open" are usually sleepy; nothing more.

However, the trouble can be with the eyes themselves. Every effort should be taken to safeguard them as they are your chief reading tool, as well as an important memory instrument. What your eyes see, they transcribe to your mind for visualization in whatever you may read.

Accordingly, when your eyes tire, check back on the factors given: Proper lighting, good reading posture, periods of relaxation, smoky atmosphere and the like. If you are wearing glasses, make sure that they are well cleaned, and keep them that way during a sustained reading session. That's like having a windshield wiper working, when you need it in driving a car.

It may be that you need glasses, if you do not already have them; or that the glasses you now are wearing may need changes. Or your eyes may need examination for some other reason. Here, again, reading proves its value. Normally, reading under proper conditions should not tire your eyes, so if it does, it is a warning where your eyes are concerned, something you might not have learned readily or as soon if they had not been challenged in this way.

Advisedly, when any of the signs of reading or associated memory fatigue arise that are in the least bit puzzling, consultation with your personal physician should be sought. It is good insurance.

Shaping
your basic
reading
mechanics
III
to speed
memory

Analysis of reading is this chapter's theme. Speed and retention depend upon recognition of reading, for which techniques are detailed. These have taken the place of time-wasting procedures that involved reading the same thing over and over in order to retain it.

Here, you are introduced to the art of "digesting" material on your own, so you can begin to read it as rapidly and effectively as an article condensed by experts. Samples of primitive "word-by-word" reading are compared with improved "duplex speed" and still more modern "triplex" and "multiplex" speeds.

Accuracy, span and speed of reading are synchronized in this discussion, showing how more can be comprehended from rapid reading because the broader coverage gives added associations. Other related major influences considered are rhythmic reading and accurate return sweeps of the eyes.

For coordinating the mechanics of word recognition and reading speed, practice charts are given. These are used in conjunction with a special device known as the Read-O-dometer. How this can be applied to test and benefit your reading ability is explained.

In acquiring or improving any skill, the first step is to analyze the processes involved. In golf, a player keeps his eye on the ball, while he gives attention to the backswing of the club, then the actual stroke, and finally the follow-through. In an automobile, the driver must watch the road, but at the same time observe the actions of other cars and be on the lookout for warning signs and red lights.

These processes not only require coordination; they bring other factors into play, sometimes with faults that become painfully apparent. The golfer, for example, may tend to slice the ball, and to correct this, he is forced to change his stance. The motorist may jam the brakes, stopping the car too suddenly, because he is slow getting his foot to the pedal.

This applies to many other actions of lesser prominence, even so slight as the efficient locking or unlocking of a front door, which can become quite a problem if you depart from your customary habit of putting the key in a certain pocket, or if you forget to change the key from another suit.

Start Analyzing
Your Present Style

In reading, it is especially important to analyze your present process. This may surprise persons who regard reading as an automatic action, or a habit acquired at a very early age. They will insist that they have progressed far in their reading, and are confident that they belong in a superior bracket.

But have they progressed as far as they should?

Or, are they like the inveterate golfer, who somehow can never "break" a hundred?

Or the driver of years experience, who still goes through occasional STOP signs?

Or the people who are always losing their keys?

Almost certainly, you may not have progressed as you should, for the simple reason that your learning to read was limited to an early period. Persons who learn early, but neglect to do much reading, find themselves handicapped when they take up serious reading, and may be forced to backtrack in order to come up to their proper level. Conversely, those who become avid readers at an early age may incline to go beyond their depth of comprehension, or improvise inefficient speed measures of their own, which may prove even worse, because corrective measures will be required.

How Speed Reading Can Help
Improve Your Reading Style

With speed reading, you can "digest" book and magazine material on your own, cutting it to about the time that an average reader would take to go through a digested article. (The latter, of course, applies to material that has been consistently condensed, not an article composed chiefly of excerpts.)

By carrying the process further, and applying it to material already digested, you can accomplish phenomenal results, stepping up your comprehension to top speed. The advantage, incidentally, of properly digested material, is that you know it is all essential. This is a slight curb on added speed, as you won't want to miss anything; but you can keep up a consistent pace, without trying to skip through inconsequential matter, since there is none.

In short, you can't become bogged down with irrelevancies, and that is a highly important factor in speedier reading, particularly when memorization is also desired. Unwieldy sentences, minor issues, and ambiguous statements all impede speed.

Once, reading was regarded as a painfully slow and exacting process, letter by letter, syllable by syllable, finally word by word. Actually, the mind does note the order of the letters, forming syllables as needed in the recognition of certain words, but the process is so instantaneous that two, three, and even more words can be read in almost a glance.

This is due almost entirely to the basic memory factor. Having memorized words through familiarity with them, the reader recognizes them on sight, and thus can instantly build them into phrases or ideas, just as words themselves are built from letters.

Thus, the primitive reader who went through the mental process of spelling it out, as "T-H-E — The, C-A-T — Cat" is really no more obsolete than the modern word-by-word reader who mentally recites "The" — "cat" — "ran" — "up" — "the" — "tree." The better way, of course, is to go after the entire idea, "The cat ran up the tree."

Using the Three-Word Method to Speed up Reading

Two points, however, should be borne in mind at the start. Recognition of individual words is basic and is part of everyone's early training, both in memory and reading. Therefore, a reader must graduate from it; and in cases where he is on very unfamiliar ground consisting of unusual words, he may revert to it.

The other point is that there is a limit to the number of words that can be observed and recognized simultaneously; hence even a comparatively simple statement may be taken in word combinations or phrases, rather than a complete sentence.

As a simple example, our sentence, "The cat ran up the tree" would be read by the "word-by-word" beginner as:

1. <u>The</u> <u>cat</u> <u>ran</u> <u>up</u> <u>the</u> <u>tree.</u>

Upon "graduating" or getting away from the "word by word" limitation, the reader would take the words in pairs as:

2. <u>The cat</u>   <u>ran up</u>   <u>the tree.</u>

Expanding the process still further, the words could be combined into groups of three:

3. <u>The cat ran</u>   <u>up the tree.</u>

Comparing these, we note that in 1 The "one-word" method, there is no real concept. After finishing the sentence, the reader must think back and add up what really happened.

In 2 The "two-word" method, we have a subject, "The cat,"

an action, "ran up," and an object, "the tree." Not only is the sentence read in about half the time; the elements can be put together promptly, with only a brief flashback.

In 3 The "three-word" method, we have two immediate pictures. "The cat ran" gives us the motive; and "up the tree" supplies the target. The sentence is read in about one-third the time and its concept is automatic.

The "three-word" method can be further extended—as will be discussed—but in many instances, such as this one, it fills its full purpose. Breaking the sentence into two components: "The cat ran—up the tree" is quite as comprehensible as the full sentence, "The cat ran up the tree."

The reason words can be read in multiples instead of units is that reading is both a physical and a mental process. By studying its mechanics, you can apply your mind to its full possibilities. The eye reads by a series of motions and pauses, not at a constantly restricted speed. This enables the eye to move faster than the plodding "letter-by-letter" or even the basic "word-by-word" process, because it is during each pause or "fixation" that a reading impression takes place.

Fixation is necessary to see the words in sharp focus. The more frequent the pauses, the slower the reading process, because the rate of recognition is reduced. The fewer the pauses, the wider the span of recognition, and the faster the process. Here, the factor of comprehension enters. Word recognition is meaningless, unless the reader comprehends the substance of what he reads. That, in turn, is vital to remembering as the follow-up of reading.

Trying the Three-Word Technique

We have given a simple example of varied speeds of reading; now, a more advanced type is in order. Let us take the opening paragraph of the Declaration of Independence, and underline it for the three reading speeds.

1. ONE-WORD PROCESS

<u>When, in the course of human events, it becomes necessary for one people to dissolve the political bands which have connected them with another and to assume among the powers of the earth the separate and equal station to which the laws of nature and of nature's God entitle them, a decent respect for the opinions of mankind requires that they should declare the causes which impel them to the separation.</u>

Here, the inadequacy of the one-word or single-speed process is definitely apparent. It is slow, it has many pauses, and its progressions are irregular. In going through it, the reader will tend to double up on the shorter words, as "in the"; "for one"; "and to"; "of the"; "to which"; and "and of." All these are steps in the right direction.

They lessen pauses, add speed, and make the progressions more even. Still better, they encourage the second stage.

2. DUPLEX SPEED

<u>When, in the course of human events it becomes necessary for one people to dissolve the political bands which have connected them with another and to assume among the powers of the earth the separate and equal station to which the laws of nature and of nature's God entitle them, a decent respect for the opinions of mankind requires that they should declare the causes which impel them to the separation.</u>

Here, the words are doubled up to a faster and more intelligible reading speed. In a few instances an extra word has been included, when it obviously should be. In this example, all the lines end in paired words, but that does not ordinarily matter. An odd word may be treated simply as a "duplex" and the reader goes on to the next line.

3. TRIPLEX OR MULTIPLEX SPEED

<u>When, in the course of human events it becomes necessary for one people to dissolve the political bands which have connected them</u>

with another and to assume among the powers of the earth the separate and equal station to which the laws of nature and of nature's God entitle them, a decent respect for the opinions of mankind requires that they should declare the causes which impel them to the separation.

Here, we find not only an effort to triple up, but to stretch the reading span to the limit. Where the doubler was content with pairing "the laws" and "of nature" in conformity with his somewhat standardized procedure, the triplex-speed reader goes multiplex with "the laws of nature." The same applies to the doubled "a decent" and "respect for," which the triplex-speed reader stretches to the multiplex form of "a decent respect for."

The Benefits of Multiplex Speeds

1. Where the single-speed plods, and the duplex-speed jogs, the triplex- or multiplex-speed races, yet absorbs ideas more effectively. Its very tendency to stretch, frees it from restraint. A combination of five short words, as *in a very big hurry* can be captured in one pause, because actually it covers no more space than a typical three-word combination, such as *it becomes necessary*.

2. That is not all. With triplex (or multiplex) speed, the reader often encounters a single word or a pair of words when he reaches the right end of the line. This leaves a shortened or unfinished "recognition span." Instead of making a pause, the reader's eyes perform a "back sweep" to the beginning of the next line. There, all as part of the same recognition unit, the reader picks up the first words at the left of the line, adding them automatically to the last words of the line above.

In the sample given, the operation of this back sweep is indicated by an underlining extended to the right of one line and to the left of the next.

Thus, broken down into "recognition units" in which back sweeps are regarded as a single "span," the reading process would consist of the units shown on page 39.

These are somewhat arbitrary and therefore may vary with different readers; but the sample as given, provides some interesting features involving memory factors, where the back sweep is concerned.

Take the first instance:

<u>for</u> . . . <u>one people to</u>

Here we have a case where the eye, upon finishing the previous span (*it becomes necessary*) picked up the word *for* and immediately went into its back sweep, fixing on the words *one people to* at the start of the next line.

That is, it caught *for* just as it might have noted a comma, or even a blank margin at the end of the line. With an experienced reader, there would be no perceptible pause. He would gather in the word *for* as a bonus and add it to the first three words of the next line, giving him four in all.

But to do that, he would have to remember the word *for,* so this is a case of instantaneous or "flash" memory.

Now, consider these:

<u>connected them</u> . . . <u>with another</u>
<u>the separate</u> . . . <u>and equal</u>

In each case, there was a short pause, a back sweep and another short pause, showing "momentary" memory, linking a partial idea to the remainder. The reader sought completion and focused upon the first two words in the next line to attain it. This was done in a slightly prolonged pause, with the back sweep included.

Next in order:

(nature's) <u>God</u> . . . <u>entitle them</u>

Here, a memory process was required to form the unfamiliar term "nature's God," which in turn was momentarily remembered for linkage with the start of the next line. Again, the reader was seeking to complete an idea, so focus on two words was enough.

MULTIPLEX SPEED READING PROCESS

When, in the course	station to which
of human events	the laws of nature
it becomes necessary	and of nature's
† for one people to	† God entitle them,
dissolve the political	a decent respect for
bands which have	the opinions of
† connected them with another	* mankind requires
and to assume	* that they should
among the powers	declare the causes
of the earth	which impel them
† the separate and equal	to the separation.

---

† Recognition units preceded by this sign are those in which a back sweep was utilized.

* Recognition units preceded by this sign were noted separately instead of using a back sweep.

The final instance:

> . . . <u>mankind requires</u>
> <u>that they should</u> . . .

Here, the last two words of the top line were sufficiently complete for the eye to finish its pause there and make a back sweep without a "carry over" of a memorized word or words. This, in turn, allowed the reader to focus on the first three words of the next line, gaining a full recognition span.

3. There is another subtle memory factor here: that of establishing one thought impression before launching on another. In addition, the reader who uses triplex or multiplex speed learns to deal in phrases as well as words, and is thus aware of what is coming up. He knows that the phrase "mankind requires" will probably be followed by "that"; and to prolong a pause to wind up with *mankind requires . . . that* would offer no advantage.

Instant Memory and Five
Major Keys to Speeded Reading

1. Accuracy of recognition. Knowledge of words and their meanings is the prime adjunct in both oral and silent reading. Readers should gain familiarity with words and phrases within the vocabulary limitations of specific subject matter; then extend this further for more difficult reading.

2. Wide span of recognition. This is the amount of wordage covered during each pause, as already described. Noting two (or more) words at a time lessens any tendency to dwell on individual words and aids in the recognition of phrases and the linkage of ideas, improving comprehension.

3. Speed of recognition. Gained through applying and increasing the wide span of recognition. By graduating from word-by-word to duplex and finally triplex or multiplex speed (as described earlier) the reader links words, forms phrases and gathers context automatically and without unnecessary analysis. Speed of recognition is the key to speed in reading, reducing the habit of too many pauses.

4. Rhythm in perceptions. This is furthered through speed of recognition. It overcomes the irregular progression found in slower reading forms. Since wide span and speedy recognition extend the degree of comprehension, idea linkage is increased, favoring a rhythmic progress from each pause to the next. The danger here is in regression, or a backward movement to make sure of something noted during a previous fixation. This should be avoided as far as possible.

5. Accurate Return Sweeps. This is an added factor that accompanies rhythm in perceptions. With narrow columns, in which fixations are few, the return sweep is almost part of the rhythmic flow. With book pages, where the lines are read clear across the page, the return sweep is proportionately longer, and therefore more exacting. If inefficient, forcing a pause before the back sweep or limiting the words noted at the start of the next line, this can usually be charged to overspeed.

Here, the memory factor comes to the fore. Bad return sweeps show that the reader is missing something. The same applies to regressions that disturb the reading rhythm. They may mean that speed of recognition is not up to par. That, in turn, can be blamed on too wide a span of recognition, either for the reader, or in relation to the material at hand. In the final analysis, the trouble may go clear back to lack of accuracy in recognition.

Often, two or three of these factors may contribute to the trouble; but memory is invariably involved, one way or the other. Either the reader slows himself through his desire to "make sure" that he is right, or he rushes ahead, taking it for granted that he knows what he is about. As a result, he underestimates his memory, or overtaxes it.

How to Construct and Use
Your Own Read-O-dometer

The physical phase of word recognition and reading speed must not be overlooked, so to coordinate it with flash or momentary memory, you can test yourself with the *Read-O-dometer,* a device

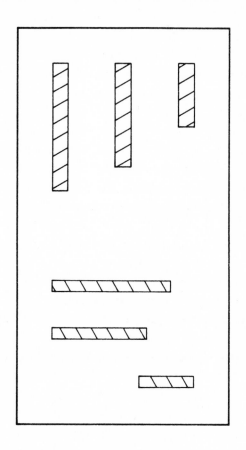

How to Make a Read-O-dometer

1. Trace above pattern onto thin postcard type cardboard, using a dull stylus, backing the page with carbon paper.
2. Cut out the shaded portions from the cardboard, to form slots.
3. Complete the Read-O-dometer by cutting along the borders of the rectangle.

READ-O-DOMETER

(These drawings not actual size)

Full size Read-O-dometer pattern for use with this chapter appears on opposite page. And a Read-O-dometer is included inside the cover of this book.

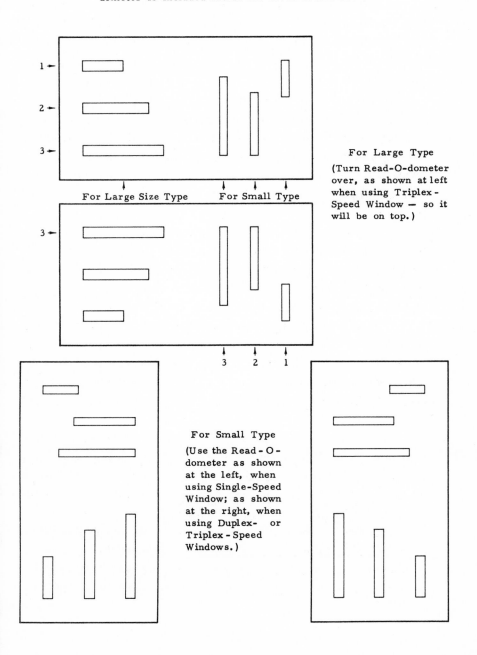

For Large Type

(Turn Read-O-dometer over, as shown at left when using Triplex-Speed Window — so it will be on top.)

For Small Type

(Use the Read-O-dometer as shown at the left, when using Single-Speed Window; as shown at the right, when using Duplex- or Triplex-Speed Windows.)

that is described fully on page 42. It is used with the columns
shown on page 45, in the following manner:

1. Start with group "A" consisting of three-letter groups or
combinations. Use the Large Type portion of the Read-O-dometer
and place it so its Single-speed window shows the word "Letters"
just above the column. Note the first "t" in "Letters." That is your
"target" letter.

2. Now, move the Read-O-dometer down so that the first
combination shows through the window. You will be sighting on
the third or final letter of the group, capturing the first two letters
with it, so that the three are taken as a unit. Immediately glance
away or cover the combination; then try to name its third letters
in their proper order. Proceed with the next combination; and so
on.

3. With the four-letter combinations, use both "t's" of the
word "Letters" as your "target," but favor the one to the right.
The aim is to keep pulling over, picking up the first letters, or
drawing them along, so to speak. With the four-letter groups, you
will find the "double letter" endings helpful, when they occur.

4. The next column consists of five-letter groups. Here, the
second "t" in "Letters" is your positive "target." To stress this, the
letter "x" is used as the fourth letter in the first section of the five-
letter groups, so you can sight on it as "target." In the later sections,
other letters appear in fourth position, but always, it is the "target"
letter.

This lessens the tendency of the eye to stress the early letters
as it moves from left to right, which is perfectly natural, since you
read in that direction. The purpose is to get away from the "letter
by letter" spelling that slows the reading of words. Training with
these jumbled letter combinations helps toward that goal.

Thus far, you can call off letter groups from memory and then
check back. This does not encourage vocalization, as with these
combinations, no actual word reading process is involved. You can
do the same with further groups, but repeating them aloud is

LETTER GROUPING CHART
FOR USE WITH THE READ-O-DOMETER

A. *Three Letters*	C. *Five Letters*	D. *Six Letters*	E. *Six and Seven letters*
djp	rjdxq	rkkxvw	dj xbh
mbf	zwgxn	gmbxyy	g kztw
ksv	mjzxc	zmzxbq	bsm jz
rkw	tlvxj	nctxtc	gb nmy
lzj	pbkxr	gswxrf	- - - - -
ntb	vwvxt	lkrxql	rztx mp
jgc	- - - - -	- - - - - -	rd xpkg
svb	mdhbm	bmkkjn	gsw bzk
qsx	bzzkr	hsrbsq	ve gfdq
B. *Four Letters*	fdgwf	vnkggv	mkt tdw
rjcc	hwkqq	pwznpc	bl mprr
pbgx	mnzzd	xtnjnh	kr wcws
kkvr	vxkrk	ljzjvk	nzjj zy
lbml	- - - - -	- - - - -	- - - - - -
dmhh	bkhsv	nmrtkj	bhgxkmn
kwzb	wjcmt	lxqkbv	krrxlqn
zvnn	cqtwr	cgbntl	mptxjpl
qmdg	kbmzh	mbscxj	bjvxmtr
bkkr	lcdjg	hdsfvn	- - - - - -
rgsw	xqmbf	gpbcxg	cggvntq
vtjv	dxjnp	txymjl	rlknvvw
kqkq	mhfzq	nzbzdp	zxhcbdd
			mptbhsw

cumbersome and means checking groups singly. So, it is better to write them on a sheet of paper as you glance at them, even beginning with the four- or five-letter groups. Then you can go right through and check back later.

5. With the six-letter groups, you can still use the fourth letter as your "target," but here you will be noting one more letter at the right. That letter makes a difference, as you must focus strongly on the fourth leter as "target" in order to include the sixth. There can be no hesitancy in the pick-up of the first three letters.

6. In Column D, the first section contains groups with "x" as the fourth and "target" letter, just as with Column C. This will help with the early combinations. After that you are "on your own" as the fourth letters vary in the succeeding combinations.

7. In Column E, spaces are used. These would occur between regular words of one to four or even five letters, which in normal reading would be grasped as a single word, when they appear together. Here, "six or seven" letters includes the space, as we are dealing with the span covered by the eye.

8. With the actual seven-letter groups, one section has an "x" as the fourth or "target" letter; in the other group, there are no special "target" letters.

When practiced, this test can increase the perception span, which is important for recognizing new or long words. It also shows how "flash" memory aids letter placement, as each time you must remember the combination long enough to check it verbally or write it down.

Using the Read-O-dometer
for Regular Reading

In regular reading, you deal with familiar words, not letter combinations as such. Hence you can identify words on sight. Again, the memory factor is at work, through recognition, which is

THREE-SPEED CHART

FOR USE WITH THE READ-O-DOMETER

Single-Speed	*Duplex-Speed*	*Triplex-Speed*
Any of	Reading this	Now you are going
these	should prove	at triplex-speed or
words	somewhat more	faster as you run
should	exacting, as	your eye down
be easy	it requires	this column of
to read	the reader to	three or more words.
because	identify two	All are common
all are	or more words	enough for you to
composed	at one time.	know. Therefore, you
of one	This is the	should be able to
or two	duplex-speed	read this column
syllables	system that	almost as quickly
and are	accomplishes the	as either of those
common	same result	that appeared before.
enough	in approximately	
for the	half the time.	
average		
reader to		
recognize		
on sight		
without		
trouble.		

always strong in any field of repeated endeavor. This allows extension of the perception to word combinations or phrases.

Again, the Read-O-dometer is used to demonstrate this.

The Three-Speed Chart appearing on page 47 consists of common sentences in vertical instead of horizontal form. The Large Type portion, Single-speed Window of the Read-O-dometer is used with Column One.

1. Simply place the Read-O-dometer so that you can move it straight down the column, causing each new word (or words) to appear in rapid progression. You will find that they register at a constant speed which is at least as fast as you can conveniently frame each line.

2. Now, shift over to Column Two.

Here, you use the Duplex-speed Window in exactly the same fashion. You will find that the same rate of speed will produce better results, as specified in the columnar statement which you will read. Any slackening will be comparatively slight. By coming back to this chart later, you will find that "doubling up" becomes almost automatic.

3. Finally, move over to Column Three, using the Triplex-speed Window.

Here, an appreciable halt may be needed with each group, but it is still the speediest process, as the development of the context is smooth and effective, lessening any hesitation in linking up ideas. Remember that the "triplex speed" is mental, and if the downward motion of the Read-O-dometer seems slow, the effect is largely relative. Don't try to speed it, or you will find yourself moving your eyes, taking in two flash impressions, left and right, which will defeat your purpose.

Compare the Speeds to Shifting Gears

Summed up, these "speeds" are like shifting gears on an old-fashioned automobile. The "single" window is your "low," which makes a big roar and pulls you out of trouble, but is slow getting anywhere and will wear you down in the meantime.

The "duplex" window is your "second" gear, gathering speed and proving highly efficient on the upgrade, when you may be climbing through some difficult type of reading. However, it has limitations and will fail to make speed on the straightaway.

The "triplex" window puts you in "high," the smoother, more effective gear for this type of steady reading, just as for steady driving. You may have to vary it, according to conditions, but in such ordinary reading you can stay with it and often ride over obstacles, without resorting to a slower speed.

When reading at "triplex," or "multiplex" speed, you are still limited by the perception span of the Triplex-speed Window. If you find that two words take up the space that three (or more) would normally require, treat those two as three. The same may occasionally apply with a single word. Take this example:

> The novel was quite bad. Its narrative
> was uninteresting and its descriptions were
> abominably redundant, turning the book
> into a masterpiece of ambiguity and utter
> incomprehensibility.

Here, you will note that the two words *abominably redundant* and the single word *incomprehensibility,* each fill the wide window, making them equivalent of the shorter three (and four) word units.

Using the "Three-Speed Chart" to Increase Perception Spans

It may seem a far cry from the recognition of a single word to three or more at a time. It would be, if we were dealing with jumbled letter combinations, like those given earlier, but even a casual reader picks up common words more easily than unrelated letters groups.

1. In Column One, the limit is nine letters to a word. By focusing on the exact center of the Single-speed Window of the

Read-O-dometer, you will hit the fifth letter (instead of only the fourth, as with the letter groups). You would recognize the word "these" by sighting the second "e." With "be easy," you would sight the letter "a," picking up the word "Be" and finding yourself in "easy."

2. Now, if you go for the sixth letter, as "d" in "should," "s" in "composed," "b" in "syllables," you will soon be picking up the letters (or word) from the left, at the same time becoming more aware of letters on the right.

3. With Column Two, you will be sighting on at least the seventh, preferably the eighth, and even the ninth or tenth letter, drawing in syllables and complete words from the left, as you take in an additional word, or part of one, on the right.

4. Thus, with Column Three, if you focus on the center of the wide window, you may not need the last few letters at the right, as you will recognize the meaning of the final word from those that you have absorbed.

For example: <u>during last November</u>

If you hit either of the last two letters in the word "last" ("s" or "t") you won't need more than the "Nov" or "Novem" of "November" to register your recognition of the full span.

5. In cases where a word "runs out" of the right side of the window, you can either pick it up as part of the next "flash," with that much of a start, or if you get the meaning instantly, you can move farther ahead for your next fixation.

For example:

In Florida, the sunshine is a great attraction.

With the Read-O-dometer, the wide window would reveal:

In Florida, the sunsh

Sighting on the comma, you could simply take it as, "In Florida, the" and slide the Read-O-dometer along to pick up "sun- shine" as the first word of the next span, so you would have:

<u>In Florida, the</u> <u>sunshine is a great</u>

Or, if your first glimpse of "sunsh" registered as "sunshine," you would simply skip the rest of the word in sliding the Read-O-dometer to the right, thus gaining a word in your next span:

In Florida, the sunshine is a great attraction.

To test this further for yourself, use the Read-O-dometer on book pages of similar type size, utilizing the "Large Type" or "Small Type" windows, as the case may be. Samples of both types are shown on page 52, so you can start your experimentation there.

Find Your Own Span—
Then Work to Increase It

The main purpose now is to determine your span of perception through recognition of words within the Read-O-dometer's various limits. That is, it gives a clearer insight into your actual reading process. You can slide it a little to the right, or back to the left, to include a word, as your eye might run along; or to hold off on such a word.

If you find that the "triplex-speed" span is too wide, use the "duplex-speed," sliding the card a little to the right, whenever you think you can squeeze in another word. As with a modern automatic gear shift, you can slip smoothly from second to third, so to speak.

When going from one line to the next, include return sweeps in this process; in short, try to gain a working measurement of your reading process. If you find yourself "between speeds," use the Large Type "duplex-speed" window on a page of Small Type printed matter. This will enable you to capture more words in a shorter span.

These tests and exercises will serve as an excellent preliminary step to the reading and memorization processes that make up our next chapter.

READ-O-DOMETER EXERCISES *

1. LARGE TYPE

When I came down from my apartment in the tree, I looked about me again, and the first thing I found was the boat, which lay, as the wind and sea had tossed her up, upon the land, about two miles on my right hand. I walked as far as I could upon the shore to have got to her; but found a neck or inlet of water between me and the boat which was about half-a-mile broad; so I came back for the present, being more intent upon getting at the ship, where I hoped to find something for my present subsistence.

2. SMALL TYPE

When I came down from my apartment in the tree, I looked about me again, and the first thing I found was the boat, which lay, as the wind and sea had tossed her up, upon the land, about two miles on my right hand. I walked as far as I could upon the shore to have got to her; but found a neck or inlet of water between me and the boat which was about half-a-mile broad; so I came back for the present, being more intent upon getting at the ship, where I hoped to find something for my present subsistence.

---

* Excerpt from The Life and Adventures of Robinson Crusoe by Daniel Defoe.

How to apply
natural memory
directly
to
IV your

reading

Here is sound advice on turning old reading habits into new. It begins with a discussion on how to break the "comprehension barrier" as a step toward rapid and efficient reading. Ways are given to supplant the old habit of vocalization by visualization. The keying of pronunciation with reading is also discussed.

Graphic examples are used showing how comprehension can be extended further to speed up reading. Unfinished words are listed so that syllables can be added mentally. Another list consists of unfinished sentences to which words can be logically and rapidly added.

Visualization is covered in detail, illustrating how "thinking while reading" helps turn ideas into actualities. Whole phrases are reduced to key-words in a sample chart, as a pattern for the comprehending reader to follow. The chapter concludes with a striking example of rhythm reading.

All reading habits may serve as memory jogs.

This is something to consider before branding certain habits as "faults" that should be summarily dismissed and shunned forever. The reading process, as already mentioned, is something that grows with you. It depends upon instant recognition with memory a basic factor, if it is to work speedily, as we want it to work.

Since the process grows with you, it is quite possible to outgrow the habits which went with slower measures. But there are times when you may have to resort to those earlier stages, and quite justifiably, as they are part of the ingrown memory and reading process.

Suppose you were staying in a house where you had gone up and down stairs a few times, but were not yet really familiar with the place. Evening arrives and you realize that to go upstairs, you need a light. So you turn one on, to make it easier.

On the other hand, suppose the electric current has been cut off. In that case, you use a flashlight or even a candle to find your way, not as rapidly, but at least effectively. However, if those are not available, you just have to grope your way through the dark, going very slowly indeed.

How "Returning to Basics" Can Prove Helpful

Reading is very much like that. Once you become reasonably proficient, the process is as automatic as walking about in broad daylight. During the early stages, you had to grope, and later on, you needed something to light the way with more difficult reading assignments. Therefore, falling back on such measures is not a form of regression, at least not when circumstances justify it.

When do such circumstances arise?

Another analogy will help to answer that question.

In this era of jet propulsion, we speak of aircraft "breaking the sound barrier." Much of today's reading is done at a "jet speed" which does practically the same thing. It breaks the "comprehension barrier." As you read, you usually absorb ideas instantaneously, once that "barrier" is broken. Naturally, while that is going on, you don't want to be handicapped by such primitive habits as vocalization and fingerpointing to what you read.

Actually, you won't be so handicapped, once you have broken the comprehension barrier; in fact, you can't be, or you wouldn't have reached that stage at all.

How to Break the "Comprehension Barrier"

Under other circumstances, suppose that you, as a jet-age pilot, encounter conditions that overtax your flying skill, or make it impossible to attain the speed required to break the sound barrier. In that case, you might perhaps as well be flying an old "prop" job or a Piper Cub, which would make landing easier.

So it is with reading. Your jet speed will be wasted, in fact harmful, if you fail to break the comprehension barrier. If you stay within range of your reading skill, this will not happen very often; but when it does, you can go back to basic training. In so doing, you may well find discarded habits helpful rather than harmful.

Here is a sentence that is like walking or even running in full daylight. One that breaks the comprehension barrier in a flash:

Now is the time for all good men to come to the
aid of the party.

You can read that in "multiplex speed," taking four words at a time, sighting on the target "dots" as indicated in the lines below:

Now is•the time for all•good men to come•to the
aid of•the party.

Or, you can ease it a little, resorting partly to "triplex" instead of "multiplex" speed, and using a return sweep because of the two lines:

Now is•the time for al•l good men to•come to•the
aid•of the par•ty.

You may recognize the above sentence as a common exercise used in elementary typing, because of the short, simple words and the variety of letters. Here is another from the same category, but a better typing exercise as it utilizes all the letters of the alphabet:

The quick brown fox jumped over the lazy dog.

This can be taken quite readily at triplex-speed with three perception spans, each attained by sighting on the central word:

<u>The quick brown</u> <u>fox jumped over</u> <u>the lazy dog.</u>

Or some readers may capture it in word groups of larger multiples, sighting on the spots indicated by the dots:

<u>The quick•brown fox</u> <u>jumped over•the lazy dog.</u>

So far, good. Not only good, but easy. Now, let's take a pair of sentences in which all the words are short and quite easy to pronounce, a passage which seemingly should come within the range of handling through instant comprehension. However, it won't, unléss you are already familiar with it; and can recognize it for what it is:

> 'Twas brillig, and the slithy toves
>   Did gyre and gimble in the wabe;
> All mimsy were the borogroves,
>   And the mome raths outgrabe.

Here, the tendency is to VOCALIZE, or at least to SUB-VOCALIZE, by imagining that you are hearing the eleven unfamiliar words pronounced. It goes back to early fundamentals, being an effort to identify words by sound as well as sight.

The excerpt is from Lewis Carroll's nonsense poem, "Jabber-wocky" in which imaginary words were coined to sound meaning-ful, sort of a predecessor to our modern "double-talk." Note their subtle similarity to actual words; "slithy" like "slimy," "toves" like "roves," "gyre" like "gyrate," "wabe" like "babe" or "wave."

When read aloud, the false word "mome" leaves you wonder-ing whether it should be pronounced like "home" or in two syllables, like "mo-me" in order to fit the meter of the verse in which "Jabberwocky" was written.

Why Vocalization Helps
in Only a Small Way

This shows how vocalization forms a reading groundwork, both in poetry—which is often meant to be read aloud—and when dealing with unfamiliar words and phrases. In short, vocalization and subvocalization have a reading value in a somewhat limited way.

Also valuable is the learning of the alphabet, and practice in building it into syllables and then into words, instead of only trying to learn reading of words as a whole. Through such building, odd words like these become pronounceable, thereby suggesting meanings.

A child who spells a word, "R-E—re, M-E-M—mem, B-E-R —ber: remember," will gradually learn to recognize it as *remember* as his reading skill increases through practice. In that point, then, he will be at least as well off as the child who has been taught to swallow and digest *remember* all as one word, and recognizes it as such.

Now put the two of them up against an unintelligible word like *Jabberwocky*. The one who can crack it into "J-A-B—jab, B-E-R—ber, W-O-C-K—wock, Y: Jabberwocky" will move right along with the words that follow, while a person using a process of "full word" recognition, may still be trying to pronounce or guess at the title.

The point here is that falling back on a primitive process like vocalization fits with what was said about going into a lower gear when driving. It is slower, noisy, and uses more gasoline, but it gets you there, when otherwise you might be stalled.

Here is another example of how memory and reading depend on one another when dealing with unconventional material. The following sentence is in French:

Je suis le capitaine de vingt-cinq soldats; sans moi, Paris serait pris.

Here, the reader will find himself in one of three general categories:

1. If he knows no French, the words will be an almost unfamiliar jargon. He will recognize "captain" and "Paris" and he may guess at a few others; but he will be simply fishing for

words. It will be like trying to learn to read all over, with need of interpretation.

2. If he has studied French in a very limited way, or has a smattering of it with some other language of Latin origin, he will read it word by word, translating each into English as he goes along, a labored process that is difficult to speed. Thus:

> I am the captain of twenty-five soldiers; without
> *Je suis le capitaine de vingt-cinq soldats; sans*
> me Paris would be taken.
> *moi Paris serait pris.*

3. If he reads French fluently, and really knows the language, he should be able to read and think in French, just as he would in English. He would catch the play on familiar words, and recognize the sentence as a riddle; namely:

The "captain" is the letter "A" which stands at the head of "twenty-five soldiers" representing the twenty-five letters of the French alphabet. Without "A," the word PARIS would become PRIS. Thus "Paris" would be "taken."

This illustration, or any other involving a foreign language, will help clarify what occurs in the normal reading process when a person is confronted with unfamiliar or little-used words or phrases.

It is interesting to note the part that vocalization plays while reading anything in foreign or technical language. If either is totally unfamiliar, the tendency is to pronounce words as they look, which may be entirely wrong.

Thus a person knowing no French (Category 1) would try to grasp the word *suis* by pronouncing it as *swiss* or *sue-is*, whereas the proper pronunciation is *swee*. Then if they heard the word pronounced correctly later, they wouldn't be able to identify it. The same would apply to a word like *pris*—properly pronounced *pree*.

Anyone with a smattering of French (Category 2) might ignore the French pronunciation and vocalize in English, as part of the translation process. Here, vocalization serves a purpose; the reading has to be slow and exact; hence repeating it in English, half-aloud, serves as verification. This is akin to classroom practice where students are required to translate aloud, so there is an added tendency to resort to it.

A person knowing French well (Category 3) might vocalize in that language, as a refresher or mode of concentration. Here, the habit might prove very bad, as faults in pronunciation would be accentuated. In short, if you must vocalize, do it properly, or you will be falling into a double trap.

We have stressed this "foreign language" example because it applies very forcibly to all unfamiliar or difficult reading, and particularly so with highly technical material. In vocalization, you are caught betwixt and between. With simple material, it is a bad habit that retards you; with complex material, you are apt to stumble and get it wrong.

Knowing When and Where to Discard Vocalization

On that account, discard it with the simple. With the complex, make sure of any vocalizing you may do. Many readers go to the dictionary to learn the meaning of a new or uncertain word, yet how many check the pronunciation? Very few, particularly avid readers, who are the persons who need it most. Every word has a meaning and a pronunciation; the two must be balanced, so that comprehension will apply to the spoken as well as the written form.

This is an important factor in association, one whereby a person can increase his speed of reading and comprehension sooner, for the more familiar you become with individual words and their peculiarities, the more quickly you can note the differences or similarities in others.

For example: The word *crustacea,* a class of shelled creatures including lobsters, shrimp and crabs. Anyone familiar with the word *panacea,* pronounced pan-a-*see*-a, might be inclined to pronounce *crustacea* as krust-a-*see*-a, upon reading it as a strange or new word.

Actually, *crustacea* is pronounced krus-*ta*-she-a, with the accent on the second syllable and the third pronounced "she" instead of "see." Now that we have settled that, consider the more commonly used word, *crustaceans,* as applied to lobsters and their kin.

It might seem that *crustaceans* should be pronounced as "krus-ta-*she*-ans" and not "krus-ta-*see*-ans." But, not so. Both of those are wrong. Due to the accent on the second syllable in *crustacea,* the word *crustaceans* becomes "krus-*ta*-shans" and another frequently used derivative, *crustaceous,* is pronounced "krus-*ta*-shus."

Avid readers often far outstrip their knowledge of the spoken word. Hence they, the very persons who have left vocalization far behind, are also ones who can use it to real advantage when exploring new realms that are replete with deceptive words whose meaning and pronunciation must both be properly pegged.

Using Finger-Pointing Sparingly

An alternative to vocalization or subvocalization is FINGER-POINTING which has also been marked as a bad reading habit that should be discarded. It should be, in most instances, though its use by some persists to a limited degree of reputed benefit.

Thus when looking up a word in a dictionary, finger-pointing may be helpful at times. This also may apply when checking the pronunciation of the very words that you have decided not to vocalize until you have them right.

During continued reading, finger-pointing is used by occasional persons in noting long and unfamiliar words, or stressing difficult phrases. This resembles the underscoring of passages in text books, which sometimes proves an aid to study.

Often, an author will make use of underlined words, or put them in italics. Similarly, the reader who finger-points may be doing this on his own, to emphasize whatever he regards as essential.

He may be doing it to help concentrate on difficult reading. On the other hand, when dealing with a long word, breaking it into visual syllables is generally preferable to vocalization or finger-pointing.

As a further example, *both* such processes—vocalization and finger-pointing—may be used, sometimes in combination when reading dialogue, as in a play, especially when committing some of it to memory. This, and the others of course, are special cases, but they show the appeal of any device that may possibly help couple reading with remembering, one way or the other.

How does this affect rhythmic reading, the process so essential to the duplex and triplex speeds that have been favored? It helps some persons, when it succeeds in furthering their comprehension, which is the great aim of rhythmic reading. Any device that does that deserves consideration, but every effort should be made to limit such slowdowns.

The greater your familiarity with the type of material that you are reading, the general nomenclature, the author's style, and other vital features, the more you can speed your reading without sacrificing comprehension. To be slow but sure in the early stages, to dwell upon "key" passages, even reading them over again if need be, may pay dividends later.

How to Handle Long Words in Speed Reading

Long words can slow both reading and comprehension, not just because they are less familiar than short words, but because they reduce the number of words in the perception span. This means that your rate of reading may be cut from triplex speed to duplex speed. Yet those long words may tell less than their shorter equivalents.

Here is a striking example of this factor. First, take the simple adage:

People who live in glass houses shouldn't throw stones.

This can be read easily at triplex speed, three words at a time, as follows:

<u>People who live</u>   <u>in glass houses</u>   <u>shouldn't throw stones.</u>

Now, note the following sentence which expresses exactly the same idea, but in longer and more unwieldy form:

Individuals inhabiting crystalline domiciles should assiduously avoid cultivating such activities as projecting fragmentary geological speciments.

If read at a relative duplex-speed, this would run:

<u>Individuals inhabiting</u> <u>crystalline domiciles</u> <u>should assiduously</u> <u>avoid cultivating</u> <u>such activities as</u> <u>projecting fragmentary</u> <u>geological specimens.</u>

In this instance, reducing from triplex to a relative duplex speed means in terms of wordage; not perception span. Actually, you will be using the same "triplex" slot for the long words as the short. This is easily demonstrated, by setting the three-word phrases in one column and the two-word combinations in another; then checking them by running the wide slot of the Read-O-dometer down each column. Thus:

SHORT WORD COLUMN	LONG WORD COLUMN
People who live	Individuals inhabiting crystalline domiciles
in glass houses	should assiduously avoid cultivating
shouldn't throw stones	such activities as projecting fragmentary geological specimens.

While this is an exaggerated example, it shows what happens when unwieldy words begin to encroach into a text. You may have to strike a 3-2-3-2-2-3 tempo instead of taking three and maybe more words in nearly every span. Seldom, however, will you be continually reduced to two words throughout.

In any case, do not try to overstretch your perception span. This was a very common mistake in the early days of speed reading. Observers watching the eye motions of readers, had noted the long moves and the main fixations. Some of the slighter moves and momentary pauses, including the regressions had not yet been detected.

How to "Digest" Half-Words

Later experiments with special cameras caught some of these lesser motions and pauses. These indicated that two and a half words of average length represented an efficient perception span for most readers. This, of course, would amount to three short words, or even more if very short.

Keep that figure "2½" strongly in mind. It can imply that in many instances, you will take in half a word. Often, you can mentally supply the rest to make a whole word and skip along to the next target.

For example:

an utter imposs	add *ibility*
a raging hurric	add *ane*
nothing so outlan	add *dish*
Antony and Cleo	add *patra*
A towering skys	add *craper*
A presidential cand	add *idate*
The Egyptian pyr	add *amids*
Department of Agri	add *culture*

All these are the result of previously developed associations, which form the strongest memory links. More important, the links are double. Each half-word is a partial key to its other half; but it also has a relationship to the words that preceded it in the same perception span. Thus you are forming and strengthening associations as you read.

Even stronger is the linkage of certain short words which are so closely allied that they become accepted phrases, almost like a complete word in themselves. Whenever you strike one of these, you naturally complete it mentally:

thunder and	add *lightning*
give the devil	add *his due*
over the bounding	add *main*
the star-spangled	add *banner*
just around the	add *corner*

On the opposite page are other lists of phrases ending in half-words, with spaces for their completion; also phrases of short words, requiring one or more, as indicated. You may find some familiar, others obscure, but in either case, try to complete them, and then check the answers that are given at the bottom of the page.

How Topical Knowledge Speeds Reading and Comprehension

This brings up two other important factors of speed reading. The first of these is TOPICAL KNOWLEDGE, or familiarity with the subject. As an example, this passage:

> The frigate *Constitution* headed out of Boston harbor and soon was sailing over the bounding (main) with the star-spangled (banner) proudly floating at her mast-head.

Notice how the historical substance of the paragraph provides added clues to the words "main" and "banner." Here, a reader of history could fill in much more. Upon reaching the word "floating," he could easily supply "at her mast-head."

Anyone familiar with a subject can speed his reading through such previous knowledge. That is highly applicable toward scholastic or technical reading. Sometimes it restricts readers to very limited fields in which they feel at home. That, of course, should be avoided. Our goal is expansion.

CHART

high school grad _ _ _ _
ride on the merry _ _ _ _   _ _ _
various religious den _ _ _ _ _ _ _ _ _
a filter-tipped cig _ _ _ _ _ _
very highly recom _ _ _ _ _ _
guilty of an indis _ _ _ _ _ _ _
they ate at a res _ _ _ _ _ _ _
A supreme court de _ _ _ _ _ _
they were very antag _ _ _ _ _ _ _
the summits of the Him _ _ _ _ _ _
many things are ins _ _ _ _ _ _ _ _ _
the answer was incons _ _ _ _ _ _ _ _ _
in the telephone dir _ _ _ _ _ _
a one volume encyc _ _ _ _ _ _ _
the capitol at Wash _ _ _ _ _ _
he answered the tel _ _ _ _ _ _
an international expos _ _ _ _ _
fighters were outnum _ _ _ _ _
held a secret rend _ _ _ _ _ _

Greatest Show on _____
beat around the _____
Stars and Stripes _____
hurry! hurry!! _____
locking the stable _____
breaking the sound _____
until we meet _____
running neck to _____
a hoard of pirate _____
sank in the Atlantic _____
rode across Brooklyn _____
five hundred miles an _____
at your local drug _____
in Springtime, grass is _____

COMPLETIONS (*column 1*)
graduate; merry-go-round; denominations; cigarette; recommended; indiscretion; restaurant; decision; antagonistic; Himalayas; insignificant; inconsequential; directory; encyclopedia; Washington; telephone; exposition; outnumbered; rendezvous.

COMPLETIONS (*column 2*)
earth; bush; forever; hurry!!!; door; barrier; again; neck; treasure; Ocean; Bridge; hour; store; green.

How Visualization
Increases Expansion

Visualization consists of the transcribing of words to actions and pictures, not only as an aid to remembering, but as an outgrowth of the living imagery that only memory itself can provide.

Think while you read. Turn ideas into visualized actualities. Stimulating this, more than anything else, is the great effect of reading, that has created a modern pantheon of fictional characters far more alive than many actual historical personages.

Why do the Three Musketeers still capture popular fancy, though their times would have otherwise been forgotten? Why do many people recall London's Baker Street, the residence of the fictional Sherlock Holmes, more readily than Downing Street, where so many factual prime ministers flourished through the years?

Simple because they, the readers, caught the mood of the written word that they absorbed, and glorified it far beyond the expectations of the authors. Readers were able to see and remember the word pictures painted by the authors. From those, they anticipated others to follow. Between times, they pictured themselves as their own heroes or heroines, or saw persons who reminded them of certain characters from those books. Thus, through their own imagery, they conditioned themselves for more of that literary diet.

Here, the memory factor induces a still more rapid assimilation of material. Readers become more and more avid: witness the hold that Charles Dickens once had upon his public; the later boom in Western novels, from the time of Zane Grey on; and the grip that fantasy and science fiction have upon present readers and will exert upon generations to come.

Aiding this visualization and serving as memory jogs are repeated bits of characterization, catch phrases—supplied by both the author and his characters—and use of special dialects which may run the gamut from a Western "lingo" to the quasi-scientific nomenclature used by imaginary interstellar travelers in a purely mythical outgrowth of the space age.

Using Visualization to Stimulate
Association and Extend Memory Span

Just as these "pages" or "props" or "what-have-you" can speed your reading while bending you to the author's whim, so can you turn simpler and less obvious phrases into pictures that can be epitomized or abridged in a single word. In such visualization, you not only recognize; you also project. This practice stimulates association, and greatly extends the memory span.

This association in turn, links up the phrases that you are reading, say at triplex speed, so that you soon begin to anticipate oncoming phrases and complete ideas. New reading will recall old, just as a few strains of music from a new song will enable a musician to remember an old song.

Later, a recollection of something read long ago will help you remember what you read just recently, but might otherwise have forgotten. Pegging new ideas as you read them is something like sorting items into bins already labeled for their reception. What you learned as a slow reader, or through frequent repetition, becomes the clearing house for the brief and sometimes fleeting impressions that you gain during speed reading.

This association may be likened to the familiar experience wherein you take a given word, say "bell" and follow up with the word-chain that it suggests. Thus one person might say: Bell—church—Sunday—rest—

Another might form the chain: Bell—sleigh—snow—reindeer —igloo—Eskimo—

These, however, are not intended to lead anywhere. They simply serve as a partial index to the working of the individual mind. On the other hand, in reading, by *thinking* as you *read,* you can turn phrases into such linked words wherein the climax is an epitomized or representative word. This is a word which in itself can be transformed into a complete picture that will incorporate the full suggestion as well as the significance of the original phrase.

Thus: "Boy meets girl" suggests the word "romance" which in turn suggests "wedding." There, you stop. Immediately, you visualize a wedding scene, hear the strains of music, even catch the scent of flowers. This may tie in with a wedding that you actually attended, or focus upon some ceremony that you saw pictured, or read about.

Whatever the case, the "boy and girl" are projected into the ideal setting of the "wedding," both expanding and strengthening the picture and the characterization. This is the *motif* found in many romantic novels and popular love stories. Whether or not the anticipation is realized, the idea rouses interest and creates suspense, thus strengthening the memory factor throughout, with due emphasis upon the actual climax.

Using Phrase-to-Word Links
for Faster Reading

On the opposite page, you will find a series of these PHRASE-TO-WORD links. Most of them follow an obvious pattern, as they should; but at that, they are arbitrary.

This chart can be used in various ways. One is to run the Read-O-dometer down the column at the left, utilizing the long slot to test your perception span and speed of comprehension where common phrases are concerned.

At the same time, you can keep the column at the right completely covered. Then, go through the phrases openly, but use the shortest slot to reveal the "key" or "focal" words one by one, guessing at them as you proceed.

Or you can simply use both columns openly, fixing on the phrase, then the focal word, and finally visualizing them interchangeably, as already described.

An Experience in Triplex-Speed Visualization

On page 71, we have an excellent piece of descriptive writing by William Dean Howells, which has been underlined for reading

CHART

Phrase	Word
boy meets girl	wedding
clash of arms	battle
two speeding cars	crash
month of May	blossoms
fine-feathered friends	birds
Transatlantic flight	vacation
when shadows fall	night
South of the border	fiesta
the five fifteen	commuter
trip to the moon	rocket
root of all evil	money
for whom the bell tolls	funeral
one last gasp	exhausted
black and white	soda
dark thunder clouds	gloom
roast beef and gravy	dinner
a penny saved	bank
the final score	game
trip the light fantastic	dance
man's best friend	dog

at triplex speed. That is arbitrary and can be varied by the individual reader, but by using our pattern, you can test your reading pace with or without the Read-O-dometer.

Note how short endings, like *It is at* which finishes Line 1, enable you to pick up the first three words, *once shoveled into* of Line 2. This is one of those quick "catch-and-carry-over" glimpses from the upper line.

Where the final words are a picture in themselves, as with *legion of poverty*, or *when the most determined*, or *of St. Mark's Church*, the eye can fix there and begin a new "start" with the next line.

In forming pictures, certain phrases are immediately linked. You start (Line 1) with an impression of narrow streets, while "fallen" and "snow" combine and are utilized action pictures of "shoveling"—"canals"—"poorly clad men" in Line 2. The scene broadens into "St. Mark's Place" in Line 3, where "music" begins an impression, which is clarified by the combining of "innumerable" and "shovels," only to strike a raucous discordance in "smote upon my ear," Line 3.

Notice the picturization of the "twilight" caused by the snow itself, the *artist's sketch* of the outlined church, with its floating effect, tying in with the *slow motion* expressed by "weary kind" and "effort in dreams."

A passage like this is well suited to reading rhythm. The use of mostly familiar words allows a wide perception span along with almost immediate comprehension; and the author's clarity of style aids both. But the wealth of his ideas, the finely etched details, make it a vivid word painting, which you may wish to admire in detail.

Having set a pace with such reading, go easy in speeding it, or you may lose the effect of your own visualization. In contrast to an action scene, where details rush you to the climax, descriptive writing draws on so many facets of the memory that there is often a justifiable inclination to linger with it.

In Venetian streets they give the fallen snow no rest. It is at once shoveled into the canals by hundreds of half-naked facchini;* and now in St. Mark's Place the music of innumerable shovels smote upon my ear; and I saw the shivering legion of poverty as it engaged the elements in a struggle for the possession of the Piazza. But the snow continued to fall, and through the twilight of the descending flakes all this toil and encounter looked like that weary kind of effort in dreams, when the most determined industry seems only to renew the task. The lofty crest of the bell-tower was hidden in the folds of falling snow, and I could no longer see the golden angel upon its summit. But looked at across the Piazza, the beautiful outline of St. Mark's Church was perfectly penciled in the air, and the shifting threads of the snowfall were woven into a spell of novel enchantment around the structure that always seemed to me too exquisite in its fantastic loveliness to be anything but the creation of magic.

That adds up to the rule: Don't speed your reading for the sake of speed alone. Give word memory a chance to play its proper part. Trite statements that jump to mind can be read rapidly, but when words conjure deeper impressions, hold your pauses and gauge your rhythm to suit.

Add speed where it counts best, applying it more as the material falls below the quality and significance that you have taken as an established standard.

---

* (*Italian*) "rabble"

How to read

and

memorize

V   word groups

more

efficiently

This chapter shows how you can expand your store of "sight words" by "word building." Prefixes and suffixes are discussed so that you can take further advantage of their role as "multipliers" where vocabulary is concerned. You will learn the value of comparisons and breaking down long words into their simpler components for improvement of your reading skill.

You will also find how you can spot "words within words" as keys to quick sighting, which is extended to the use of key-words in "sight phrases." From examples, you gain patterns that you can utilize in other reading. These show you how speed induces speed, with catch phrases actually keying themselves. Descriptions that you are able to condense quickly from lengthier wordage also show how unneeded words can be rejected. The ways for you to select and form mental images of word pictures will be impressed here.

An opportunity is given for you to use the Read-O-dometer in noting "sight words." Flash cards are described, and ways for taking advantage of them for rapid recognition of words and phrases.

So far, at every step that you have taken to improve your reading skill, you have probably become increasingly aware of words that you have recognized on sight. If you could take an accurate count, you might find that you have greatly multiplied your "sight words," as these are aptly termed. Despite this, you should not stop there, for the larger the increase, the better your reading vocabulary becomes.

Every word that jumps up as you see it, striking you as an old friend, is another aid to rapid reading. It not only adds itself to your store, it helps you to remember more, because you can concentrate on new or less familiar words that you may encounter from now on.

Word Building with
Prefixes and Suffixes

One important adjunct to gaining "sight words" is the process of "word building." You can cultivate this through a study of prefixes, which precede words, giving them special meanings, and through suffixes, which provide significant endings.

Take the word *decided.* Put the prefix *un* before it, and you have *undecided, or not decided.* Change *decided* into *decision* with the suffix *ion,* and you have something *decided upon.* Again use the prefix *in*—as a variant of *un*—and you have *indecision, or the lack of ability to make a decision.*

Thus by adding a prefix and suffix, while cutting down slightly on the basic word, you turn a seven-letter word into a ten-letter word, and in so doing give it the significance of an eight-word phrase!

On pages 76-77, you will find lists of prefixes and suffixes, with sample words derived from them. Some are from the Latin, others from the Greek, and some are of plain English origin. In those respects, there is no need to differentiate between them here, as they are now part of the English language and can be learned by comparing them with other English words.

At the same time, you must watch for exceptions. The prefix *ad* signifies proximity, as in the word *adhere* or *adjoin*, but the word *adder* is a snake, having no connection with the prefix.

Similarly, you must watch for conflicts. There was the case of a man who looked through a dozen dictionaries for the word *agenarian*, but never could find it. The reason was, he had come across the word *nonagenarian*, and thought that it was something that was *not agenarian*, just like someone who was nonsectarian, or nonpartisan, the prefix *non* meaning *not*.

However, nonagenarian comes from the Latin *nonagenarius*, meaning "consisting of ninety," and now denotes a person between ninety and a hundred years of age. The prefix *non* happens to be nonexistent in that case!

Also, forms from two languages may combine into a single English word. One example is nonagon, a nine-sided figure, from the Latin *nonus*, or ninth, and the Greek *gonia*, or angle. The word automobile is another maverick, with the Greek *auto*, for self, combining with the Latin *mobile*, or moving, to mean self-moving.

In your study of prefixes and suffixes, you must again apply the three elements coupled with association, namely, interest, attention, repetition, in order to get results. As you do so, you should find every stage of that process smoother.

Discovering word forms useful in word building naturally rouses interest. The mere comparison of words with similar forms demands attention. The farther you go with it, the more intriguing it can become, and the factor of repetition strengthens the whole procedure. You will be amazed how words literally form themselves and how well they stay in mind, speeding reading in the meantime.

How far can this word building be carried? Right up to one of the longest words in the English language, which happens to be *antidisestablishmentarianism*. A real sockdolager, until you reduce it to simple terms, starting with the word *establish* that shows plainly in the center.

a	at, in, on, as afloat	mis	wrong, as mispronounce
ab, abs	from, as abdicate or abstain	non	not, as nonsense
ad, ac, af, etc.	to, as advance, accede, affix	ob	toward, or opposed to, as observe, or obstacle
ambi	both, around, as ambiguous	out	beyond, as outnumber
amphi	both, around, as amphitheater, amphibious	over	above, as overburden
		per	through, as perforate
		post	after or later, as postpone or posterior
ante	before, as antedate	pre	before, as prepaid
anti	again, as antitoxic	pro	forward, in favor of, as proceed or propound
be	make, as belittle		
bi	twice, as bicycle		
cata	down, as cataract	re	back, again, as return or revive
circum	around, as circumvent		
con	with, together, as confer	retro	backward, as retrograde
contra	against, as contradict	se	apart, as seclude, separate
de	down, from, as descend or depart		
di, dia	twofold, as dilemma	semi	half, as semifinal
dis	apart, not, as disagree or disassociate	sub	under, as submarine
		super	above, over, as superintend
en, em	in, as enter, emplace	syn, syl, sym	with, together, as synonym, syllable, symphony
epi	upon, among, as epidermis or epidemic		
ex	out, from, as exit or exclude	trans	across, through, as transport or transparent
extra	beyond, as extraordinary	ultra	beyond, as ultramarine
fore	before, as foresee		
hemi	half, as hemisphere	un (in)	not, as undesirable
in	in, into, as inject	under	below, as underfed
in (un)	not, as inconsiderate	vice	instead of, as viceroy
inter	between, as intercept		
meta	beyond, as metaphysical		

* Many words also serve as prefixes, for instance *self* as in self-explanatory. Noting the occurence of such words as prefixes is a great aid in word-building.

COMMON SUFFIXES*

able	inclining to, as capable		places, as bacteria or America
age	state or process, as tonnage or passage	ian	practitioners or inhabitants, as musician, Parisian
an (ane, ain)	belonging to, as Grecian, mundane, terrain	ic	pertaining to, as gigantic or basic
ance, ence	an activity, as performance, existence	id	a quality, as acid
ary	occupation or place, as secretary, armory	ine	a compound, as chlorine
ary	pertaining to, as customary	ion	a process or state, as in action, position, tension
al	pertaining, as musical	ish	a similarity or relationship, as childish, greenish
ant, ent	an operative force, as valiant, student		
ate	agency, as pirate or delegate	ism	a result, as realism
		ist	one who practices, as pessimist
ate	verbal form, as desecrate	ive	belonging to, as receptive
dom	condition or control, as kingdom		
en	small, as mitten	less	lacking, as fearless
en	quality, as golden or broken	lent	fulness, as violent
		ly (like)	having the quality of, as softly, quickly
er	belonging to, as farmer, New Yorker	ment	a condition, as amusement
er	comparative, as larger	or	a state or action, as error, governor
et, ette	small, as puppet or marionette	ous	displaying a quality, as anxious, officious, vicious
est	superlative, as greatest	some	
ess	feminine suffix, as hostess		a resemblance, as gladsome
ful	imbued with, as hopeful	tude	state or condition, as magnitude, gratitude
ia	names of classes or	ward	direction, as outward
		y	condition, as difficulty

---

* Many lesser suffixes or variations go into word formation. In looking for examples, any exceptions should also be noted.

From that came the word *establishment,* using the suffix *ment,* meaning a fixed form of government with an established church. Through the prefix *dis,* anyone opposing that called for *disestablishment.* Such a person became a *disestablishmentarian,* by adding *ian,* and his policy was called *disestablishmentarianism,* thanks to the suffix *ism.* Then along came people who opposed all that, and used the prefix *anti* to proclaim *antidisestablishmentrianism,* with themselves as its upholders.

A long word, but quite expressive if you take a deep breath before breaking it into its syllables. As a sight word, you can recognize it at a glance, once you are familiar with it, for there is no other word quite like it.

Look for Words within Words

Often, you can recognize as many as a dozen compounded words by sighting a single "key" word that is common to all, as *sensational, sensatory, insensible, nonsensical, sensitive* and others built upon the word *sense.*

Where such "keys" are not available, you may often sight a "word within a word" and link it to the longer word by a phrase, thus forming a sight word through association.

Whenever words key as well as those just given, it is convenient to take advantage of them. In other words, you can strain some portion of a word into a key, or link it in some way that will jog your memory, but you must be careful that it does not defeat its purpose.

For example, you could remember the word *flamingo* as a *Flaming-O,* but still keep in mind that its pronunciation is fla-*min*-go.

The word per*pend*icular is keyed to *pend,* which means to hang as if balanced. Noting that, you will never misspell it "pin" instead of "pen," as some people do. But you must treat *pend* as a key, not an accent, or you may mispronounce the full word.

Similarly, *inspired,* can be keyed as in*spire*d, with a graphic mental picture of a *spire* pointing to the sky. However, a switch

Character—char*act*er—act.

You can *act* the part of a char*act*er in a play.

Intelligent—in*tell*igent—tell.

An in*tell*igent man can *tell* you things.

Posterity—*poster*ity—poster.

A theatrical *poster* may interest *poster*ity.

Swindler—s*win*dler—win.

A s*win*dler can *win* all your money.

Brotherhood—br*other*hood—other.

Members of a br*other*hood help each *other*.

Presentiment—*present*iment—pre*sentiment*.

A *presentiment* is a foreboding of the future that
    may result from a *present sentiment*.

Radishes—ra*dish*es—dish.

Ra*dish*es are served in a *dish*.

Terrain—*terra*in—ter*rain*.

Terra is earth, *rain* is water, and you find both
    in every *terrain*.

Carrousel—car*rouse*l—rouse.

The loud noise of a car*rouse*l will *rouse* everyone.

to in*spira*tional shortens the "i" in *spira* and puts the accent on the "a," making the pronunciation inspi-r*a*-tional.

The advantage of a short "key" to a long word is that you get to know the long word and its vagaries. Whether the key is real or artificial, the result is the same; in fact, if it is far-fetched but of your own origination, it is often better. In any case, its oddity links it to other oddities in spelling, pronunciation, and definition. Thus it starts a chain reaction in the form of mutual associations.

Using Key-words in
Sight Phrases

Just as a long word can be keyed by a "word within," so can a group of words be keyed from a single word. Sighting the key-word means recognizing the group. Here, you are dealing almost entirely with familiarity gained through sustained or repeated reading.

A word, or a pair of words, keeps popping up from a group, so that whenever you see it in a sentence, the rest of the phrase springs to mind. This was discussed and stressed in an earlier chapter, so you will quickly recognize the process when applied in full. The following example shows how a few word combinations can be keys to an entire group:

> In order to comprehend all that you read in full, you should make it a practice to dismiss any other thoughts entirely from your mind, so that you can concentrate solely on the subject that is immediately at hand. There are three general rules that may prove helpful in such cases, namely:
>
> 1. Seek quiet when you read, so that your surroundings will be free from any disturbances or undue interruptions.
>
> 2. Make sure that you are in a proper mood for reading, so that inward disquiet will be as absent as any outside annoyance.
>
> 3. Make a careful choice of the subject matter, so that your reading interest will be sustained over the customary period.
>
> Those three rules add up to real results that will become increasingly apparent the longer you adhere to them. With your average reading, you will find that you catch the gist of things so rapidly that ideas actually flash to mind.

The total number of words in those paragraphs comes to more than one hundred and fifty. Now, suppose you go through it with an eye for key words and their accompanying phrases, boiling it down to this:

> Comprehend all . . . . you read . . . . dismiss . . . . other thoughts . . . .
> Concentrate . . . . Three rules . . . .
> Quiet . . . . proper mood . . . . Choice of subject matter . . . . Real results . . . . Flash to mind.

Less than twenty-five words from the original statement, or just about one-sixth, tell the story. If you could have spotted these instantly, you would have read the passage six times as fast.

How Speed Reading
Increases Speed

Now, actually, in rapid reading, you do exactly that. The "in-between" words are reduced almost to the status of mere punctuation marks. By actual count, you may take in fifty or so, nearly double the essential twenty-five, but as you sight those surplus words, you reject them. So they do not add much to your total reading time.

On the contrary, if you try to read all one hundred and fifty words, you will be slowed by the lesser phrases. Each sentence, instead of flashing a quick, single thought, will offer contrasts that must be weighed. The sentence construction will also inject itself into the pattern, slowing the process still more.

Why are these longer, fuller, and perhaps somewhat ponderous sentences needed?

They are needed partly for the plodding reader who uses all those extra words; and they are also required to give the passage its full sense. A series of only disjointed phrases would merely slow you, and demand more time. Writing is often done that way, caption style, to make readers halt and eye each item. This is apparent in the contents pages of a book.

The writer's use of extra words and rounded phrases makes rhythmic reading possible at different speeds, enabling each reader to attain his peak. It is somewhat like pushing the speed of a car to its limit on a turnpike, resulting in better time than by taking a rough short-cut.

Catch Phrases That
Key Themselves

In an earlier chapter, various word combinations were listed, all leading to rapid reading due to their familiarity. Such catch phrases automatically speed the process. Here is a paragraph specially composed of familiar phrases. Go through it rapidly, then check it by the marked passage that follows shortly.

> During the long cold winter, Jim's long cherished ambitions had approached the vanishing point. He was still giving his full and undivided attention to all forms of outside activities, far beyond the call of duty. But despite his constant, patient willingness to meet every outrageous demand that was thrust upon him, his ceaseless and untiring efforts had gone totally unnoticed and unrewarded. With every resource utterly exhausted, he came to the stark realization that he had reached the end of the line.

Reduced to simple terms, an experienced reader would gather from this passage that:

Last winter, Jim's hopes faded. He went the limit to meet demands, but was ignored and finally gave up.

Again, that cuts the passage down to about one-sixth of its original size. In its final form, it is reduced to impressions gained from reading the complete statement. The writer stated one thing, rather elaborately. You, as the reader, digested it to what might be termed a comprehensive equivalent. Adherence to the original nomenclature is unnecessary; the real purpose of the writer is to *convey* the idea, and yours is to *receive* it.

If this results in a translation of elaborate and somewhat stylized phraseology into brief and direct terms, so much the better. In using well-known expressions, the writer is literally keying his statements for the benefit of the astute reader. In this case, the phrases can be checked as follows:

> During the <u>long cold winter,</u> Jim's <u>long cherished ambitions</u> had <u>approached the vanishing point.</u> He was still giving <u>his full and undivided attention</u> to all <u>forms of outside activities.</u> But despite his <u>constant, patient willingness</u> to <u>meet every outrageous demand</u> that was <u>thrust upon him,</u> his <u>ceaseless and untiring efforts</u> had gone <u>totally unnoticed and unrewarded.</u> With every <u>resource utterly exhausted,</u> he came to the <u>stark realization</u> that he had reached <u>the end of the line.</u>

In each underlined phrase, you aim to hit a key-word that tells you enough to jump ahead. It could be that the *cold* would be enough to skip over "winter" so that the next key, *cherished*, would imply "ambitious." A jump through "approached" to *vanishing* would make "point" a word that could be skipped.

A jump through "full" to *undivided* would immediately include "attention" and a passing notice of "forms" would strike *outside* and leave "activities" for granted. The word *patient* implies "willingness," and *outrageous* can only mean "demand."

Thrust is a key to "upon him" and *ceaseless* obviously means "untiring efforts." Anything *totally unnoticed* must be "unrewarded," and the very word *resource* suggests that it is "utterly exhausted." With *stark* as the key to "realization," it is apparent that *the end* would apply to "the line" and perhaps a great deal more.

Interest, Familiarity, and Check-backs as Phrase Aids

With different readers, these keys will vary. Some may catch the first word of a phrase as an indicator of the rest. Others may skip past a word or two and pull up with the whole sense on the next word. The main point is that you go hop, skip, jump, noting the high spots and bridging the low gaps between. You are charting your own course to a degree, as your interest in the material, your familiarity with the phraseology, even your purpose in reading it at all, may determine your procedure.

The first example given was an explanatory statement pertaining to reading itself. Since it fitted into the theme of this book, interest and familiarity stood about even. You should be able to take such passages in rapid style, increasing speed as you get further into a subject. Some check-back may be needed in cases where you miss a salient point.

The second example was chiefly a test of phrase recognition. Interest in the material itself was virtually nil. You might class the interest purely as curiosity to see how well it worked. Familiarity was the great factor because the phrases were specially chosen to speed the reading process. No check-back appears necessary.

Here is a third example where interest is the prime factor. It is a piece of fine descriptive writing by John Ruskin, a master of the English language, whose prose is naturally an attention getter. The theme is simple and direct, so you will find familiar words and phrases in the text, but none appear there purposely. Give it a speed reading, hitting the high spots:

> In a secluded and mountainous part of Styria, there was, in old time, a valley of most surprising and luxuriant fertility. It was surrounded on all sides by steep and rocky mountains rising into peaks which were always covered with snow and from which a number of torrents descended in constant cataracts. One of these fell westward, over the face of a crag so high that, when the sun had set to everything else, and all below was darkness, his beams still shone full upon this waterfall, so that it looked like a shower of gold. It was therefore, called by the people of the neighborhood, the Golden River.

From the word *secluded*, you can jump straight to *valley*, then *fertility*. The words *peaks, snow, torrents* form a continuity which ends in *sun* (or *sunset*) followed by *waterfall* and *Golden River*. These "keys," when mentally rearranged, complete the picture of:

A fertile, secluded valley amid rocky peaks whose snow-fed torrents formed a waterfall that caught the sunset's glow and was called the Golden River.

Forming Word Pictures as You Read

In this case, the condensed description loses the fine flavor and nicety of expression found in the original. Still, even at a slow reading rate, the italicized sentence is just about the impression that you will retain. Terms like "luxuriant fertility," "constant cataracts," "crag so high," "all below was darkness," are rich with meaning, but grow into the picture almost of their own accord, if you allow your imagination full play.

There is, of course, the question of how well a reader can visualize a description if he reads it rapidly. Anyone who has been in a mountain valley or has seen a picture of one, should grasp the impression quickly, but it is still up to the author to portray the scene not only adequately, but in fine detail.

It is then your job, as a reader, to determine how closely you must follow the description. If you can increase speed and still keep your reading keyed to the authors' imagery, so much the better. Usually, reading of this sort, if sped up, demands a check-back to make sure that the word-picture has etched itself fully in your mind. If you find that you missed something, slacken enough to put your further reading in tempo with the author's expressions.

In the Ruskin passage just given, there is a clarity of style that helps toward easy reading. Since you now have the feel of it, go on with the next paragraph from the same story. In this case, you can time yourself, by glancing at the second hand of a clock or watch before you start and after you finish.

Or you can have someone else do the timing. The purpose is not to race through the paragraph and try to set a speed record. Such a practice is bad, and even to be conscious of the time factor is sometimes detrimental to proper reading. Just approach it casually, to determine an average speed which you can use for later comparison.

Speeding Your Tempo
as You Proceed

Here is the next paragraph:

> It was strange that none of these streams fell into the valley itself. They all descended on the other side of the mountains, and wound away through broad plains and by populous cities. But the clouds were drawn so constantly to the snowy hills, and rested so softly in the circular hollow, that in time of drought and heat, when all the country round was burnt up, there was still rain in the little valley; and its crops were so heavy, and its hay so high, and its apples so red, and its grapes so blue, and its wine so rich, and its honey so sweet, that it was a marvel to everyone who beheld it, and was commonly called the Treasure Valley.

This speeds itself as it goes along, going from *streams* to *other side* and *wound away*. The words *clouds, hollow, drought, rain, crops*, all form a sequence from which you can practically skip clear to Treasure Valley.

We say "practically skip" because such an action, too, must be "keyed" and in this case, the word *hay* enables you to "take off." If you catch *apples* as you are speeding up, you might go right on through *grapes, wine, honey,* and *marvel* to land smack in *Treasure Valley*, as if ending a skip jump.

How Words Flash Their Meaning

You simply catch "flashes" of those words as you go along, and the "pairings" of *hay—high, apples—red, grapes—blue, wine —rich, honey—sweet*, give you double cues that wave you through. Since each item is given a descriptive equivalent, the words themselves are fully stressed, as if each had been repeated or underlined.

There is more to it than that. In Shakespeare's plays, the dialogue was arranged so that the final line of a scene was in the form of a couplet, or rhyme. That was the "cue" for other actors to come on stage. The break in the blank verse—as caused by the couplet—snapped them into action.

Here, Ruskin's pairings have done the same thing in reverse. All the eye needs is the presence of a single word to slow its sweep through that chain of doublets, and it meets it in the word *marvel*. Even there, the eye does not have to stop, for the end of the paragraph is close and supplies two capitalized words that literally sum the pairs just given: *Treasure Valley*.

Choosing Reading Material
for Improvement

You can apply this process to various types of reading and test both your comprehension and your speed while you do so. No sound purpose would be served by giving extensive examples here, because it is better that you choose your own, for two reasons.

● First, you may have preferences or purposes in certain reading, so the memory factors, from *attention*, through *interest* and into *repetition*, will be more strongly activated.

● Second, as you continue your reading through an entire book, or articles of a similar type, you can begin to analyze the speed factor to see how it can be improved. Your aim is to read faster and remember more, but that should be done with some foresight.

Don't take material so easy that you can skip most of it. At the same time, avoid anything too difficult or technical, as it will demand too much attention and will disturb your reading rhythm. Novels should be avoided if they are heavy on dialogue, as most novels are today. Besides, they are apt to absorb your full interest if you like them, and they are liable to lag if you don't. Many people, when they read a story, reach a point where they rush on through, or practically go to sleep.

Material of a somewhat informative nature lends itself to reading speed tests. Classic examples would be Mark Twain's fascinating *Life on the Mississippi*, or Thoreau's philosophical *Walden*. There are many modern books that suit this purpose, particularly some of the popular condensed versions now obtainable. Those are usually geared for easy reading, which in turn makes them suitable for rapid reading.

Key-Words as Keys to Memory

In all reading, you should remember something of what you read, or there would be no purpose in reading at all. The question is, how much should be remembered and for how long. That varies according to circumstances, so the question will be answered in later chapters, when we discuss types of reading and the aims involved. One thing, however, is certain from the start. Temporary memory can be prolonged and even built into the permanent type.

This is specially true of key-words. If you can spot them as such, the more rapid your reading will become. You may pause on such words or review them; some may even be tabbed in process, as an actor memorizes his lines. This depends upon the importance of the material you are reading, and will be discussed under heads of "specialized reading" and "memory systems."

In any case, you must recognize a word to use it as a key, and you must also recognize it in order to reject it. As an example, take this sentence:

> When *history* is traced *far back* through *antediluvian* times, it invariably brings us to *primordial* man, whose *desires* and purposes must therefore be accepted as the *starting point* for whatever followed.

Obviously, "history," "far back," "desires" and "starting point" can be important keys. But there are two fairly unusual in-between words that may belong in that same category; namely, *antediluvian* and *primordial*. In fact, one must be a "key," so the question is which?

Literally, *antediluvian* means "before the Flood," referring to the Deluge of Biblical times. Thus, it can also be defined as "ancient" or "earliest." If you know that, you can immediately reject it as a key, because *far back* has already covered the case, making *antediluvian* a mere embellishment.

By a process of elimination, that leaves *primordial* as a "key." It is defined as "first in order" or "earliest in origin" or simply as "primitive." On that account, it fits perfectly into the scheme of things. From that sentence, you will remember that "history began with primordial man" which shows how a key-word is a key to memory.

Remembering Keys for
Reference and Recognition

There are times when you must pause in reading and check strange or doubtful words with the dictionary. Often, you can merely tab them for future reference, or pick them up later by glancing back over what you have read. With important reading, it is frequently a good plan to write down such words as you go along.

Whenever you do look up a word, fix it in mind as firmly as you can, adding any associations that will help. Just skipping over "antediluvian" and forgetting it because you happen to recognize "primordial" is not sound policy. Next week, you may be reading something where *antediluvian* is the key. If you check a word when you reject it, then you will have it when you need it.

Once you embark on a word hunt, you should make the most of it. Earlier, we mentioned that you can go beyond the dictionary and pick up more definitions or word associations from a thesaurus. The quest can be carried still further through a volume of familiar quotations.

As an example, a dictionary will define the words *tide* and *time*. A thesaurus will list the expression *the tides of time*. A book of quotations will tell you that *Time and tide wait for no man* and have many other references as well. All these are valuable adjuncts to reading faster and remembering more. What you have learned beforehand may spring to mind when you strike a key-word, thereby clinching a memory link with what you are reading now.

Increasing Your Capacity
for Memorization

At first approach, the continual adding of key-words to a memory store may seem formidable, but such is not the case. The more words you can recognize, the better you can remember them. Not only that, word structure becomes increasingly familiar, so that recognition itself is speedier.

Consider it in terms of objects rather than words, and you will realize the factors that are in your favor. Every day, you see new things by the dozen. If you visit new places, you will see unfamiliar faces and scenes. You remember many of these new things by associating them with old ones, or in some cases, by associating them with one another. If you add them up at the end of the day, you will be astounded at the capacity of your memory for new things.

This was taken advantage of by the famous French conjuror, Robert-Houdin, more than a century ago, when he trained his son to work with him in a mind reading act. As a preliminary, he stopped by a shop window and told the boy to note the objects that he saw there and remember as many as he could. Later, Robert-Houdin had the boy call them off.

Two things developed from repetitions of this test, using other shop window displays. Not only did the boy's listings become more accurate, as Robert-Houdin had anticipated, but he was able to call off *more objects* than before and do it in *less time*.

Thus he increased both his capacity and his speed, which you can do with the same test. The old benefactors of association—interest, attention, repetition—are at work, and in addition you will become more observant. You will note oddities about objects that will enable you to check them more rapidly and you will also tend to compare them, which is helpful.

What about the shop windows you noticed yesterday or last week? Naturally, you will begin to forget them unless you go by them regularly to refresh your recollections. Then you will find that your memory is not only sustained but improved. You will remember the old windows better while memorizing the new.

The same applies to words. Go over the lists of those that are important to remember, checking spelling, pronunciations and definitions as required. They, too, will fall in line.

Utilizing the Read-O-dometer
for Flash Recognition

We have already described the use of the Read-O-dometer as a device for increasing word span, aimed at speeding your reading. It can also be used for flash recognition of words. Set your Read-O-dometer at the top of the column appearing on page 92, and run it down, word by word, allowing only a brief flash of each.

Call off the words as you do this, or write them down if you are checking spelling. If you want to carry the test further, type or print out other lists and use a Read-O-dometer with them. This is a good team test, with one person doing the calling and the other the checking.

Two lists are given on page 92, one with "key" syllables or letter combinations in the center of each word, serving as a "word within a word" for quicker recognition. These are not essential, but can be included if helpful. With words of your own choice, try to form your own "inner clues" whenever you find them needed.

Formation and Use of
Flash Cards

Instead of using the Read-O-dometer with columns of words, you can make up "flash cards" for word recognition. These are simply typed cards, about the size of playing cards. A key-word is typed on one side—with or without an inner clue—and its definition, obtained from a dictionary, is typed on the back, with any other relevant data.

Put a stack of these cards together like a pack, all with the word side down. Turn the stack face up, then face down again, all in one quick action, so that you see the word on the bottom card, but only in a flash. Call it off or write it down, then draw out the bottom card and place it on top of the stack, still face down.

You will now be looking at the definition of the word you just called, and it will tell you whether you are right. If you want, you can make a double action of this. First call off the word on the bottom card; then define it before moving the bottom card to the top. In either case, once you have moved the defined word to the top, you will have another bottom card all set to repeat the test.

Flash cards have certain advantages, in that the words can be printed boldly so that they are visible at a distance and the cards can also be shuffled, changing their arrangement. In that way, it

LIST OF FLASH WORDS

in*si*pid	Something may taste *insipid* if you *sip* it.	insipid
re*bell*ion	The ringing of a *bell* may declare a *rebellion*.	rebellion
opp*rob*ious	To *rob* a person is an *opprobious* act.	opprobious
inde*fat*igable	No one can be *fat* and also *indefatigable*.	indefatigable
des*pic*able	To *pick* on a person is very *despicable*.	despicable
mag*nan*imous	Anyone named *Nan* is apt to be *magnanimous*.	magnanimous
com*pat*ible	Anyone named *Pat* should be *compatible*.	compatible
out*rage*ous	He goes into a *rage* at any *outrageous* suggestion.	outrageous
tu*mult*uous	A sound when *multi*plied becomes *tumultuous*.	tumultuous
com*bus*tion	The motor of a *bus* operates by *combustion*.	combustion
ins*tru*ment	If it is *true*, an *instrument* is good.	instrument
occu*pa*tion	A person gets *pay* from his *occupation*.	occupation
appre*hen*sion	A *hen* is a creature that often displays *apprehension*.	apprehension
sol*ariz*ation	The sun must *rise* for *solarization* to occur.	solarization
inter*rog*ated	A *rogue* is apt to be *interrogated* by police.	interrogated

is useless to memorize their order, something which you may do unconsciously with a column of words.

A Window Flash Device

As a special device for use with flash cards, you can make a window envelope out of heavy paper, the window consisting of a slit high enough and wide enough to show a word on a flash card. The envelope itself must be large enough to hold a stack of the cards. A flap is attached to the front lower edge of the envelope, by means of any adhesive tape. It is made of cardboard and fixed to swivel up and down.

Start with the flap closed, then swing it down and up, all in one quick action, thus gaining a glimpse of the front card inside the envelope. Try to recognize the word in that momentary flash, then draw the card out and read the back. You will be set for the next card, using the flap for another flash glimpse.

Phrases can be used instead of single words, both with ordinary flash cards, and in conjunction with a window envelope.

Tachistoscopic Tests and Their Equivalents

A special device called the tachistoscope has been designed to produce the same results as flash cards, but on a grander and more efficient scale. It is a type of projector that flashes words and phrases. The metronoscope is a similar device, but more elaborate as to presentation of phrases.

Both of these devices can be set for time intervals, so the duration of the flashed word or phrase can be reduced to split seconds. Something of the same result can be accomplished with a home projector, though not with such exactitude. These devices are useful for a number of purposes.

They make it possible to gauge the members of a group, when determining ability at flash recognition of words and phrases. With an appropriate control mechanism, they can lessen the duration of a flash to what might be termed the irreducible minimum.

This makes tachistoscopic equipment excellent for classroom aids and for scientific surveys. Though they have been credited with increasing the reading speed of certain groups in a surprisingly short time, conflicting reports exist as to the general applicability of the results obtained. For individuals inclined to mechanical gadgetry, use of a tachistoscopic aid may provide a successful incentive to development of speedier and remembered reading.

Impressions of Key-Words on the Subconscious

The "irreducible minimum" as applied to mental impressions of flashed words is almost a misnomer, for it refers to the vanishing point of conscious awareness. That is, below that level, the words may become "unseen" much as a supersonic sound is "unheard."

Such a concept has led to consideration of television programs in which certain words were flashed so quickly that nobody recalled seeing them, yet may have registered on the minds of the viewers.

These "subliminal impressions" may not be as strong as some would like to believe. They may be taken to imply that ideas can be picked up visually somewhat with the rapidity of thought itself, and stored away almost automatically. This, in turn, could be applied to account for how the reading process can be sped far beyond the average rate.

Whatever the explanation, many skilled readers gather a remarkable amount of impressions in less than a passing glance, helped by their familiarity with words, style and general context of material. How they can turn this to still greater advantage will be discussed in the next chapter.

Choosing

and

pacing

your reading

VI

to remember

more

> Proper timing of your reading speed is vital to well balanced *reading* and *remembering*.
>
> For your convenience, the various forms of reading materials have been divided into four general types: Pleasure, Cultural, Informative, Self-Improvement. The first three will be discussed here in detail, each with a specially selected example as a pattern.
>
> Through these, you can estimate your reading speed and analyze each procedure after completing it, using a list of questions and answers. Tempo is featured for the discussion of pleasure reading; rules are crystallized for the cultural type; and six "helpers" are included with the informative style.

There is an old saying that "the proof of the pudding is in the eating," and this applies to reading as well as to cooking. At the outset you should know something about the material you intend to read, just as with a dish that you plan to cook. You must give each due attention as you proceed. Toward the finish, you check back, doing a little sampling or tasting to make sure you have it right.

Naturally, there are some kinds of reading that are almost automatic, and this applies to cooking, too. They are just as simple as boiling eggs, but even there you have to watch the clock to make sure you don't take them out too soon or let them stay too long. This analogy is particularly appropriate where speed reading is concerned. If you hurry it, you may miss important points. If you dawdle, you may find yourself placing too much stress on inconsequential statements. Therefore, the trick is to give it just the right amount of time, like soft-boiled eggs.

Some types of reading—like cooking—are more complex. The "sight" words and phrases discussed in the previous chapter are like the ingredients used in concocting a special dish. The more you familiarize yourself with them, the better the comprehension and the more savory the taste.

You pick up your reading as you would a recipe. If the material or style is new or unfamiliar, you must be watchful, as you would in cookery. Even trivial factors can serve as "keys." Such words as *now, thus, also, moreover* are like adding pinches of salt or a dash of seasoning, while the stew goes on cooking.

When you come to *however, otherwise* or *in contrast,* special attention is needed, like turning over the eggs or flapjacks. If you strike *in conclusion, as a result* or simply a warning *but,* it may be time to take the roast out of the oven. Even punctuation marks can encourage speed, alert you to a change, or slow you down, according to their subtle indications.

It would be possible to make many other comparisons where reading is concerned, such as driving a car—which was mentioned earlier—or going about your daily work. The important thing is, that when speed is the issue, you must balance reading and retention. Often, they work in inverse ratio, so one should not be sacrificed for the other. In cases where exposure to the reading itself is the prime objective, you can open the throttle wide, as retention may be of little consequence. On the other hand, where remembering is highly essential, never hamper it by reading too rapidly.

Speed and Its Timing

Speed must be regarded as a means of improving reading, not as an end in itself, or it simply becomes a race. Some readers are able to time themselves on short "runs" almost at the start, and thus check immediately for guidance as to results. For others, speed may become a mental hazard that can defeat its real purpose. Slurred reading, like slurred speech, can crowd out the factors of comprehension and retention.

Timing of reading, to be meaningful, has to take account of the memory factor in balance. Anyone reading faster and remembering less is traveling in the wrong direction. A good way to time yourself is on a long-range basis. Start off by reading something that will capture your attention, and simply make a note of the time when you start. When you come to an interruption, or decide to rest, check the number of pages that you have covered.

Then, under similar conditions, with an equal amount of comparable material, do the same again. Check your time to see how much faster you read. Also note approximately how much you remembered in each case. If you are gradually reading faster and remembering more, you will be attaining your dual objective. Always, there is some element of memory involved, which should be stressed along with time saving. If you speed your reading efficiently, your memory gains will even increase that rapidity.

Ignore the urge for "speed, speed and more speed," the "faster, *faster,* FASTER" which has become a fetish in some circles. Speed can become disconcerting if you go out of your way to clock it. You may be much better off putting the extra effort into establishing memory "pegs," as covered in a later chapter. At present, however, you are still concerned with physically speeding your reading, but without straining yourself in the process.

When balancing reading with remembering, there are two extremes to be considered. In certain types of reading, if you can speed the process while keeping your present rate of retention, you will be accomplishing your main aim. In other cases, if your reading speed remains the same, but your memory span increases, you will be hitting the bull's eye in the required target.

Usually, you must strike somewhere in between, as there is always some element present of speeded reading with remembering, as well as expanded remembering with reading. Nevertheless, extensive reading does not necessarily increase vocabulary and further memorization unless it is properly applied. In turn, the application depends greatly upon the type of reading involved.

General Types of Reading

Reading can be classed in four general types, as follows: 1. PLEASURE, 2. CULTURAL, 3. INFORMATIVE, 4. SELF-HELP. Although these may be variously subdivided, they represent chief categories for speed and memorization studies here.

In each case, three general factors apply, namely, noting the material overall, the actual reading, and the check back. Since the prime purpose is to speed the reading process, the emphasis should be placed on this. However, since the other activities are essential to the effectiveness of the speed factor itself, they require special consideration, which will be covered with each category.

Pleasure Reading

This is the most popular type of reading and therefore is "made to order" for speed. Unless you have already reached your peak with it, which is unlikely, you can increase your speed with a few tries. In doing so, there is a tendency to skip passages, ignore difficulties and drop loose ends. As a result, many persons who consider themselves avid readers are not really succeeding at all in their reading.

Two factors that figure in such failure are *unfamiliarity* and *impatience*. You must first get the feel of the author's style and purpose, so you can "sight" everything from simple words to catch phrases. That, in turn, can eliminate the careless reading that results from impatience.

In pleasure reading, the reader himself is almost complete master. Obviously, unless his reading gives him pleasure, it is no longer pleasure reading. Once it becomes burdensome, it should be dropped.

Being well acquainted with the subject of a book is very helpful where speed is concerned because it contains the type of material that a reader can absorb more rapidly. That, of course, depends upon the reader himself, and even if he likes it, he may encounter pitfalls, because it becomes too easy a form of reading. If it is worth reading at all, some of it at least is worth remembering, yet there are many persons who apparently remember nothing that they read. You can check that for yourself, by taking a survey of friends who are inveterate readers, asking them what they think you should read—and why.

Often, their recollections of their recent reading will be quite vague. At other times, where their memory of it is sharp, it may have obliterated other books that they should have remembered. Years ago, when people in some ways had too much more time on their hands, this began to be called "escape reading" as it took the reader from the realm of reality and plunged him into the domain of fiction.

That may still apply in juvenile reading and fields of fantasy, but today, a large number of people are yearning for more reading time. One look at the store windows with hundreds of paperbacks where there used to be mere dozens of hard covers, is a supporting clue.

In view of the foregoing, even though you read for pleasure, you should at least gain some profit from it.

How to Turn Pleasure Reading into Profit

In pleasure reading, if you are already familiar with the author's style, you can usually plunge right into it. That is profitable for the author, whose great objective is to build himself a reading public. But is it profitable for you? Not very, if you simply play "follow the leader" with everything you read. Soon, you may tire of that author and start looking for another.

The better way is to catch the author's mood and establish a rapport. Try to feel that you are listening to a speaker or watching a drama, rather than simply perusing a printed page. Soon, you will be noting subtle points that you otherwise would have missed. Actually, you may slow your reading at the start, but you will gain so much more from it that your new insight will soon enable you to speed beyond what you may have thought was your capacity. Then you will begin to profit.

What happens when you encounter new authors? Your increased insight will enable you to apply the speed process in their cases as well. All the verbal cues and catch phrases will come to your aid. You won't have to go into deep analysis of the author's style; that is the kind of thing that may slow you. Instead, you will learn to hit the high spots and turn the whole thing into a test of speed.

Testing Your Speed
at Pleasure Reading

As an outstanding case where speed can be applied, we are taking a highly popular story of its day, *Gallegher* by Richard Harding Davis. We are using the opening paragraphs of what is a classic in its field, but was sufficiently dated so that it is now new to many readers. Not only that, it has an unusual style that can be quickly tabbed.

It has an easy flow, because it starts in the first person plural, goes to the first person singular, and then to the third person singular, so it draws you along with it. Also, it deals directly with a person named Gallegher, as the title implies. Those are all the pointers you need to plunge into it, so get started and move swiftly, then check back when you are finished.

> We had so many office-boys before Gallegher came among us that they had begun to lose the characteristics of individuals, and became

merged in a composite photograph of small boys, to whom we applied the generic title of "Here, you"; or "You, boy."

We had sleepy boys, and lazy boys, and bright, "smart" boys, who became so familiar on so short an acquaintance that we were forced to part with them to save our own self-respect.

They generally graduated into district-messengers boys, and occasionally returned to us in blue coats with nickel-plated buttons, and patronized us.

But Gallegher was something different from anything we had experienced before. Gallegher was short and broad in build, with a solid, muscular broadness, and not a fat and dumpy shortness. He wore perpetually on his face a happy and knowing smile, as if you and the world in general were not impressing him as seriously as you thought you were, and his eyes, which were very black and very bright, snapped intelligently at you like those of a little black-and-tan terrier.

All Gallegher knew had been learnt on the streets; not a very good school in itself, but one that turns out very knowing scholars. And Gallegher had attended both morning and evening sessions. He could not tell you who the Pilgrim Fathers were, nor could he name the thirteen original States, but he knew all the officers of the twenty-second police district by name, and he could distinguish the clang of a fire-engine's gong from that of a patrol-wagon or an ambulance fully two blocks distant. It was Gallegher who rang the alarm when the Woolwich Mills caught fire, while the officer on the beat was asleep, and it was Gallegher who led the "Black Diamonds" against the "Wharf Rats" when they used to stone each other to their hearts' content on the coal-wharves of Richmond.

I am afraid, now that I see these facts written down, that Gallegher was not a reputable character; but he was so very young and so very old for his years that we all liked him very much nevertheless. He lived in the extreme northern part of Philadelphia, where the cotton— and woolen—mills run down to the river, and how he ever got home after leaving the *Press* building at two in the morning, was one of the mysteries of the office. Sometimes he caught a night car, and sometimes he walked all the way, arriving at the little house, where his mother and himself lived alone, at four in the morning. Occasionally he was given a ride on an early milk-cart, or on one of the newspaper delivery wagons, with its piles of papers still damp and sticky from the press. He knew several drivers of "night hawks"—those cabs that prowl the streets at night looking for belated passengers—and when it was a very cold morning he would not go home at all, but would crawl into one of these cabs and sleep, curled up on cushions, until daylight.

Besides being quick and cheerful, Gallegher possessed a power of amusing the *Press*'s young men to a degree seldom attained by the ordinary mortal. His clog-dancing on the city editor's desk, when that gentleman 'was upstairs fighting for two more columns of space, was always a source of innocent joy to us, and his imitations of comedians of the variety halls delighted even the dramatic critic, from whom the comedians themselves failed to force a smile.

But Gallegher's chief characteristic was his love for that element of news generically classed as "crime."

Not that he ever did anything criminal himself. On the contrary, his was rather the work of the criminal specialist, and his morbid interest in the doings of all queer characters, his knowledge of their methods, their present whereabouts, and their past deeds of transgression often rendered him a valuable ally to our police reporter, whose daily feuilletons were the only portion of the paper Gallegher deigned to read.

In Gallegher the detective element was abnormally developed. He had shown this on several occasions, and to excellent purpose.

Questions on
Gallegher **Paragraphs**

Without going back over the material just read, see how much you have remembered by filling in spaces below the following questions. Skip any that you have trouble in recalling, as this is not a test, but simply a check of relationship between reading and remembering:

1. What kind of office-boys were there before Gallegher came?

   (a) —————— (b) ——————

2. What did former office-boys generally become?

   ——————————————————

3. What points were mentioned about their new attire?

   (a) —————— (b) ——————

4. Name two features of Gallegher's build.

   (a) —————— (b) ——————

5. What was the constant expression on his face?

   ——————————————————

6. What animal did he remind you of?

_____

7. With what two historical facts was Gallegher definitely unfamiliar?

   (a) _____ (b) _____

8. What was on fire when Gallegher rang the alarm?

_____

9. What were the names of the two gangs in Richmond?

   (a) _____ (b) _____

10. In what part of what city did Gallegher live?

    (a) _____ (b) _____

11. What was the name of the newspaper where Gallegher worked?

_____

12. What were drivers of late cabs called?

_____

13. What kind of "acts" did Gallegher put on?

    (a) _____ (b) _____

14. What type of news was Gallegher's chief love?

_____

Appraisal of Answers with Analysis

Since this is "pleasure reading," there is no reason why your answers to the above questions should be anywhere near 100 per cent. If you hit one or two subheads under Question 1, you hardly need to answer Questions 2 or 3 at all. Question 4 should be answered, at least in simple form, while 5 is fairly important, but 6 less so.

Questions 7, 8, 9 are unimportant, though you should be passingly aware that such subjects were mentioned. Question 10, is more important, but 11 and 12 mean nothing. Questions 13 and 14 are definitely important to the story.

Even if you miss some of the more vital questions, you can pick them up as you proceed. Gallegher, Philadelphia, the *Press* and crime are mentioned frequently as the story proceeds. Often, in pleasure reading, rejection of certain points is as allowable as acceptance, provided that you are aware enough of them to note if they are repeated.

Observe how the author has used eye-catchers to help the reader. He gets in *Gallegher* as an immediate key-word. He stresses *sleepy, lazy, bright,* by using the word *boys* after each, with the added definers, "smart" in quotes. (Question 1.) Reference to *district-messengers boys* (2) and *blue coats* with *nickel-plated buttons* (3) are on the off-beat, as noted.

Again, the name *Gallegher* crops up as a key to his description *short* and *broad* (4) which are immediately given some elaboration so the reader will note them. His *smile* (5) is amply described, as are his eyes, producing the simile of *a black-and-tan terrier* (6).

The key-word *Gallegher* again brings you to the question of his ignorance, where the examples of *Pilgrim Fathers* and original *States* (7) have capital letters as eye-catchers. Similarly, *Woolwich Mills* is a capitalized term (8) and so are *"Black Diamonds"* and *"Wharf Rats"* which are doubly stressed with quotation marks (9).

With *northern part of Philadelphia,* there is a capitalized name (10) and the same applies to *Press,* which is also italicized (11). The term *"night hawks"* has quotes to make sure you see it (12). Then, Gallegher is linked with the *Press*'s staff to introduce his *clog-dancing* and *imitations* (13) as further character delineations. Finally *"crime"*—in quotes—is stressed as his chief love (14).

Samples of Key-phrases

Speedy reading is helped by such key-phrases as *But Gallegher; And Gallegher had attended; I am afraid . . . that Gallegher was not.* Finally, comes the summarizing paragraph, brief but pointed, which plunges the reader into the story. Thus, you can use a skimming process in the early stages of such a story, setting the pace that you can follow later.

Note that there is just one unusual or little-used word in the entire passage, namely "feuilletons." It is a French word meaning small items in a daily journal. Being definitely foreign, it might have been italicized, *feuilletons*, but even there, the author was considerate of the reader, for if italicized, it would have caught the eye, whereas it is actually unimportant.

Writers of an earlier period were more literary in their choice of words. In his *Fall of the House of Usher*, Poe begins with a first person account of an approach to a sinister and melancholy house located on the brink of a black and lurid tarn, or mountain pool.

A few paragraphs later, the story runs as follows:

> Shaking off from my spirit what must have been a dream, I scanned more narrowly the real aspect of the building. Its principal feature seemed to be that of an excessive antiquity. The discoloration of ages had been great. Minute fungi overspread the whole exterior, hanging in a fine tangled web-work from the eaves. Yet all this was apart from any extraordinary dilapidation. No portion of the masonry had fallen; and there appeared to be a wild inconsistency between its still perfect adaptation of parts, and the crumbling condition of the individual stones. In this there was much that reminded me of the specious totality of the old wood-work which has rotted for long years in some neglected vault, with no disturbance from the breath of the external air. Beyond this indication of extensive decay, however, the fabric gave little token of instability. Perhaps the eye of a scrutinizing observer might have discovered a barely perceptible fissure, which, extending from the roof of the building in front, made its way down the wall in a zigzag direction, until it became lost in the sullen waters of the tarn.

Analysis of Poe's Passage

In the paragraph just given, the details are so interwoven that it is difficult to analyze it on a "question and answer" basis. The length of the paragraph itself is a forewarning of this, and each succeeding sentence stresses that the material is of a descriptive nature.

So it is largely a case of catching "key-words" such as *spirit, dream, feature, antiquity,* or indulging in a process of "phrase-hopping" as *discoloration of ages, Minute fungi overspread, fine tangled web-work, No . . . masonry . . . fallen, still perfect adaptation, crumbling condition,* and so on.

After a harrowing experience within the house itself, the narrator goes into this concluding paragraph:

> From that chamber, and from that mansion, I fled aghast. The storm was still abroad in all its wrath as I found myself crossing the old causeway. Suddenly there shot along the path a wild light, and I turned to see whence a gleam so unusual could have issued, for the vast house and its shadows were alone behind me. The radiance was that of the full, setting, and blood red moon, which now shone vividly through that once barely discernible fissure, of which I have before spoken as extending from the roof of the building, in a zigzag direction, to the base. While I gazed, this fissure rapidly widened— there came a fierce breath of the whirlwind—the entire orb of the satellite burst at once upon my sight—my brain reeled as I saw the mighty walls rushing asunder—there was a long tumultous shouting sound like the voice of a thousand waters—and the deep and dank tarn at my feet closed sullenly and silently over the fragments of the "HOUSE OF USHER."

Analysis and Linkage
of Final Paragraph

Here, questions are more in order, as:

1. What was the weather like outdoors?

   _____

2. What caused the wild light on the path?

   _____

3. What was the appearance of the moon?
   (a) _____   (b) _____   (c) _____
4. What provided a fierce breath?

   _____

5. What did the tumultuous shouting sound resemble?

_____

6. Where did the fragments of the house vanish?

_____

The answers, which are listed below can all be quickly gathered by a reference to the paragraph itself, but even that is not likely to be needed. Why not? Because the mere fact that "Questions and Answers" are applicable here depends on the summarizing quality of the paragraph itself.

Its reference to the weather, the causeway and the path, the house and its shadows, all refer to descriptive data that the author wove in earlier. To make sure that the reader will not miss, Poe openly reminds him of the "barely discernible fissure" extending downward "in a zigzag direction."

This is found in both the paragraphs quoted, in almost the same phraseology. In the first example, the description of the house winds up with reference to the tarn; in the second case, the tarn provides the final note. This is a striking example of Poe's masterful ability to interweave description with narration, all contributing to his greatness as a story-teller.

Thus, the questions themselves are almost self-answering even to the most rapid reader, provided he has learned to note repeated references or summarized descriptions.

Here are the answers: 1. Story. 2. The moon through the widening fissure. 3. (a) full (b) setting (c) blood red. 4. The whirlwind. 5. The voice of a thousand waters. 6. Into the deep, dank tarn.

Speed, Rhythm and Tempo

Now, a more technical question arises, namely: Why not apply the close but rapid process of "triplex-speed reading" to these paragraphs of Poe's? This was recommended as a good exercise with the Read-O-dometer, in connection with the Howells' description near the end of an earlier section (page 71).

The answer is, you can do so. Not only that, you will find it quite as valuable and as enlightening with Poe's graphic paragraphs. The opening sentences of the final paragraph would naturally break into phrases thus:

> From that chamber, and from that mansion, I fled aghast. The storm was still abroad in all its wrath as I found myself crossing the old causeway. Suddenly there shot along the path a wild light, and I turned to see whence a gleam so unusual could have issued, for the vast house and its shadows were alone behind me.

All forms of reading can be treated in this fashion and often should be. In short, the techniques that you have gained should not be discarded, but applied whenever advisable or required. In many cases, you can start by sighting word groups, then going into a skimming process if you can.

If such skimming is controlled, it will speed your rhythm in cases—like many of Poe's tales—where the author keeps giving you reminders as he speeds his own tempo. This either means that you read faster as you progress, or that once you have attained the proper rhythm, you will gather or absorb more as the tempo increases. That is the great secret of pleasure reading.

Cultural Reading

Perhaps you have heard the quip, "What is the difference between a fiddle and a violin?" The answer, in case you don't know it, is "The player."

An analogy can be drawn between pleasure reading and cultural reading. The difference between the two is essentially the author. This, of course, can be extended to cover the particular style that he has adopted, or the material he uses.

Checking back, the *Gallegher* excerpt is good story telling, but it can not be classed as beyond pleasure reading. Certainly it is not cultural. Poe's *Fall of the House of Usher* is a truly fanciful tale, and is definitely pleasure reading for those who delight in the macabre. But for that same specialized type of reader, it can be accepted as cultural, too, as it paints pen pictures of the weird and gruesome.

Howells' *Snowfall in Venice* is cultural reading since it is almost entirely description, but that does not rule out the story-telling factor from the cultural department. The classics teem with adventure from Homer's *Iliad* and Vergil's *Aeneid* through the works of Shakespeare. Hence many historical novels may be classed as cultural as well as popular reading. As examples, here are some passages from *Ivanhoe,* by Sir Walter Scott, which may be used to set a reading pace:

> The door accordingly was opened; and the hermit, a large, strong-built man, in his sackcloth gown and hood, girt with a rope of rushes, stood before the knight. He had in one hand a lighted torch, or link, and in the other a baton of crabtree, so thick and heavy, that it might well be termed a club. Two large shaggy dogs, half greyhound half mastiff, stood ready to rush upon the traveller as soon as the door should be opened. But when the torch glanced upon the lofty crest and golden spurs of the knight, who stood without, the hermit, altering probably his original intentions, repressed the rage of his auxiliaries, and changing his tone to a sort of churlish courtesy, invited the knight to enter his hut, making excuse for his unwillingness to open his lodge after sunset, by alleging the multitude of robbers and outlaws who were abroad, and who gave no honor to Our Lady or St. Dunstan, nor to those holy men who spent life in their service.

As with Poe's narrative, this is strong on description, but Scott has dealt more with fact than fancy, drawing a true portrait of a hermit and his surroundings during the period covered by the novel. It has words little used today, as *girt, sackcloth, rushes, link, crabtree,* so it demands a closer reading than more modern or more imaginative writing would. The same applies even more expressly with the following:

> Rebecca could not only see what passed beyond the precincts of the castle, but also commanded a view of the outwork likely to be the first object of the meditated assault. It was an exterior fortification of

no great height or strength, intended to protect the postern-gate. The castle moat divided this species of barbican from the rest of the fortress, so that, in case of its being taken, it was easy to cut off the communication with the main building, by withdrawing the temporary bridge. In the outwork was a sally port corresponding to the postern of the castle, and the whole was surrounded by a strong palisade. Rebecca could observe, from the number of men placed for the defense of this post, that the besieged entertained apprehensions for its safety; and from the mustering of the assailants in a direction nearly opposite to the outwork, it seemed no less plain that it had been selected as a vulnerable point of attack.

Here, closer attention to detail is needed, as the castle scenes are more difficult to visualize than the hermit's hut. Before embarking on such reading, it is often a good plan to study up on a period. After finishing a chapter, various points can be reviewed and checked, such as the construction of a Medieval castle and its component parts.

Exercise in Cultural Reading

Philosophical works are a strong branch of cultural reading. Appropriately, one of the greatest arguments for such reading is found in Thoreau's *Walden*, expressing his philosophy on that very subject. To show that such reading can be easy as well as cultural, key-phrases have been underlined to speed the reading pace:

> No wonder that <u>Alexander carried the Iliad</u> with him on his expeditions <u>in a precious casket.</u> <u>A written word</u> is the <u>choicest of relics.</u> It is something at once <u>more intimate</u> with us and <u>more universal than</u> any other <u>work of art.</u> It is the work of art <u>nearest to life</u> itself. It may be <u>translated into every language,</u> and not only be read but actually <u>breathed from all human lips;</u>—not be represented on canvas or in marble only, but be carved out of the breath of life itself. The symbol of <u>an ancient man's thought</u> becomes <u>a modern man's speech.</u> Two thousand summers have imparted to the <u>monuments of Grecian literature,</u> as to her

marbles, only a <u>maturer golden and autumnal tint,</u> for they
have carried their own serene and celestial atmosphere into
all lands to <u>protect them against</u> the <u>corrosion of time.</u>
<u>Books are the treasured wealth</u> of the world and the fit <u>in-</u>
<u>heritance of generations</u> and nations. Books, the oldest and
the best, <u>stand naturally and rightfully</u> on the <u>shelves of</u>
<u>every cottage.</u> They have no cause of their own to plead, but
while they <u>enlighten and sustain</u> the reader, his common
sense <u>will not refuse them.</u> Their authors are a natural and
irresistible <u>aristocracy in every society,</u> and, more than kings
and emperors, exert an <u>influence on mankind.</u> When the
illiterate and perhaps <u>scornful trader has earned</u> by enterprise and industry his coveted <u>leisure and independence,</u>
and is admitted to the circles of wealth and fashion, <u>he</u>
<u>turns inevitably</u> at last to those still higher but yet inaccessi-
ble <u>circles of intellect</u> and genius, and is sensible only of the
<u>imperfection of his culture</u> and the vanity and <u>insufficiency</u>
<u>of all his riches,</u> and further proves his <u>good sense</u> by the
pains which he takes to <u>secure for his children</u> that <u>intellec-</u>
<u>tual culture</u> whose want he so keenly feels; and thus it is
that he becomes the <u>founder of a family.</u>

Two points should be noted above; namely, that the writing
has a fullness that makes it possible to move from phrase to phrase,
but at the same time, the importance of its message cannot be
gained through a mere skimming process. Other factors, too, must
be considered in cultural reading.

Rules of Cultural Reading

From an analysis of these examples, the rules of cultural reading include the following: 1. Good preliminary choice of material.
2. Setting a pace according to the importance or the **familiarity**
of the material. 3. Pause at the end of each section or paragraph
for suitable mental review.

All these will vary with different readers. A person acquainted with history or eager to know more about it can attain a pace in such reading equal to his pleasure reading speed. The same applies for the philosophy-minded reader, and for others engaged in their favorite cultural pursuits.

On the other hand, if choice becomes careless, if speed is pushed too far, and no later consideration is given to the material itself, the value of cultural reading is lost. This is evidenced in modern science fiction, where readers often begin with a realistic approach to the space age and wind up by steeping themselves in fantasy.

Variety of Informative Reading

In simplest form, informative reading applies to the common newspaper story which can be scanned rapidly, filed mentally, or forgotten, as desired. From the start, newspaper writers are drilled in telling who, what, when, where and why, as soon as they can, even if they have to do it in only half a dozen lines.

This "spilling the beans" makes scanning easy, but the story itself may suffer. Nor can it be accepted as a criterion, because few writers—other than journalists—adhere to such rules. Therefore, it is up to the reader to ferret out the main points of such informative reading, by applying the necessary rules of his own.

Here, memory comes in immediately. The newspaper man will remember his rules, for he will be out of work if he doesn't. But the reader needs something more to jog his memory. A verse always helps in remembering something, such as one from Kipling, that included an added factor:

> I keep six honest serving men,
> They taught me all I knew.
> Their names are What and Why and When
> And How and Where and Who.

With these "helpers" in mind, you can improve your comprehension where informative reading is concerned. You must allow for the fact that they hop around a bit, and often one or another will work overtime. In any event, you can always call on the one which is most readily available.

WHAT—WHY—WHEN—HOW—WHERE—WHO

Here is a case where the six helpers can be applied to reading of much greater importance than the average news story; namely, in a paragraph from Gibbon's great work on *The Decline and Fall of the Roman Empire.*
The paragraph runs.

> The authority of the new sovereign had been ratified by the cheerful submission of the senate and provinces. They exulted in their unexpected deliverance from a hated tyrant, and it seemed of little consequence to examine into the virtues of the successor of Caracalla. But as soon as the first transports of joy and surprise had subsided, they began to scrutinize the merits of Macrinus with a critical severity, and to arraign the hasty choice of the army. It had hitherto been considered as a fundamental maxim of the constitution, that the emperor must always be chosen in the senate, and the sovereign power, no longer exercised by the whole body, was always delegated to one of its members. But Macrinus was not a senator.

The six helpers immediately evidence themselves in the following progression:
1. WHAT? The authority of the new sovereign and its ratification.
2. WHY? Because of unexpected deliverance from a hated tyrant.
3. WHEN? As soon as the first transports of joy and surprise had subsided.
4. HOW? The hasty choice of Macrinus by the army as opposed to the constitutional method.
5. WHERE? The choice of emperor should always have been made in the senate.
6. WHO? A member of the senate should be chosen and that eliminated Macrinus.

These have been listed in their regular order to emphasize the helpers, but as already specified, that could be varied. In actual practice, you take them as they come.

Informative Reading Summarized

Just as pleasure can be linked with cultural reading, so can cultural reading be linked to informative reading. Scott's *Ivanhoe* can be pleasure reading for those who like novels; it is cultural reading for those who seek literature; and it is informative reading for those who want historical facts, though there, it becomes somewhat supplementary.

Similarly, Gibbon's *Decline and Fall* might be pleasure reading to the few, but cultural reading to the larger reading public, and a positive "must" for students who are seeking the accurate historical information which such a unique work may provide.

Reading and Remembering—
for Self-Improvement

The final category in this general treatment is reading of the self-improvement type. This has an overall implication, because any type of reading can aid an individual toward self-improvement, provided it is judiciously applied.

More specifically, there is a domain of "self-improvement" through reading, which involves the acquiring and retaining of definite facts and concepts, usually those of vital importance to the reader. This constitutes a special subject wherein reading is geared even more strongly to remembering. It will be covered separately in the next chapter.

Special formulas for self-improvement reading

VII

These next pages tell you how the simpler types of reading, *pleasure, cultural,* and *informative* combine toward self-improvement which embodies all three.

Individualism is recommended as the keynote of self-improvement in reading, and the four steps of *Selection, Expansion, Learning, Finishing,* give you the key-word SELF. You will recognize how this is applied to reading faster and remembering more.

Overall reading techniques are detailed in the final portion of this chapter, starting from the simplest and continuing through those than can be utilized in methods of study as well. Each of these systems carries its own memory jog as will be given.

Reading for self-improvement covers a wide range. In a true sense, it is fundamental, for self-improvement begins with learning the alphabet, or the recognition of such simple words as c-a-t for "cat." At the opposite extreme, self-improvement can represent the ultimate in reading achievement.

The higher the attainment of the individual, the more it can be attributed to the ability to read for self-improvement. That is almost an invariable rule. Not only that, the urge continues in proportion to the attainment. Persons who have gained results through reading for self-improvement seldom have time to waste on any other kind.

Why Memory Is the Key to
Self-Improvement Reading

This only stresses the fact already mentioned, that reading for self-improvement may embody any or all the types previously discussed; namely, reading for pleasure, cultural reading, and informative reading. In fact, it is difficult to think in terms of self-improvement without including one of those.

A question, then, can be raised:
What is the key to reading for self-improvement?
The answer is definite:
The memory factor.

Without memory, there is no improvement. If whatever is read is not retained, at least in part, nothing is gained.

Actually, there is a loss, in terms of wasted time that could have been applied to reading something else with possible better likelihood of results. Proper application, though important in itself, has for its aim, memorization. In other words, the real goal of self-improvement is reading to remember, as a principal instrument.

It was once claimed that anyone familiar with the Bible and Shakespeare would have the requirements of a liberal education. Yet, without that purpose in mind, namely, the desire for self-improvement through such sources, the claim would be empty.

Many children annually read or are instructed in Biblical passages without absorbing any of their deeper significance. Similarly, Shakespeare is discussed in school rooms, quoted in classes and promptly forgotten. In short, both the Bible and Shakespeare can be treated superficially, and anything so treated will fail to make the proper impression.

At the opposite extreme, there are persons who can glibly

recite scriptural quotations, giving the book, chapter and verse, without appreciating the meaning of what they quote. In the same category are Shakespearian actors, who can fill complete parts with all the required gusto, yet who are otherwise uneducated and actually learn nothing from the roles they play.

In the first case, there is no effort to remember. Hence, little if anything is retained, so there can be no self-improvement. In the other example, all the effort is focussed on memorization alone. The substance is ignored and so is self-improvement, unless the ability to rattle off something in parrot fashion can be regarded as a real achievement.

No memory on one hand; no self-improvement on the other. Evidently, the answer is to steer a course somewhere in between, balancing the two factors, or combining them to their mutual advantage. That is reading to remember.

Let us go back to the previously discussed types of reading; for pleasure, culture, and information. In a way, they are tied to the three factors applied to association: *interest, attention, repetition*. Reading for pleasure requires interest. Cultural reading demands attention. Information, to be properly pegged, depends on repetition.

Pleasure, culture, information, all are helpful in reading for self-improvement, which in turn involves memory greatly. In its turn, memory depends upon interest, attention and repetition, which influence the first three respectively, and thus complete the circuit.

Steps That Serve as "Keys" to Self-Improvement

Individualism is a foremost essential to self-improvement, because the individual person is most concerned. If anything should be left to personal choice, it is this type of reading. Recommendations can be very helpful and should always be considered, but the rest is up to you. That gives us the keys to reading of the self-improvement type.

THE FIRST STEP: SELECTION

• *Selection* is the first key. With such a wealth of reading material available today, the very first thing to do is check through it and see what you can best use.

This does not cast discredit upon recommendations. Actually, they may be vital, as they form a guide to initiating selections. But they should be used as such. Dont' get enthused over anything just because somebody says to read it. Make sure that while enjoying it, you will be getting something more from it.

Selecting material for cultural reading demands a definite tie-in with other elements. Once you read it solely for its own sake, or to get done with it, you may miss its real message. Usually, it is supposed to give you pleasure and provide you with information as well as culture. What is more, you need those as the memory tags to retain the cultural material.

Otherwise, you may be like the commuter who decided to acquire culture by reading all of Shakespeare's plays in installments during his daily train rides home from work. He carried his pocket Shakespeare with him and was careful not to get so absorbed that he would miss his station.

He completed the project successfully, but years later, when he tried to list the characters in some of Shakespeare's less known plays, he was unable to recall any of them. What he did remember perfectly were the names of all the stations along the branch line on which he commuted.

Selecting informative reading material is perhaps easiest of all. Unless the information captures your attention and can hold your interest, there is usually no need to delve into it. Of course the important exception is study reading. Techniques for this will be described later in this chapter.

THE SECOND STEP: EXPANSION

• *Expansion* is the next step. Once you have chosen the best type of pleasure reading for yourself, expand it. Weigh results and continue with whichever is most productive. This has a reverse twist, as it prevents you from becoming "grooved" in purposeless reading simply because you like it.

With cultural reading, expansion is a "must." Poetry is an example of cultural reading that can be expanded into pleasureable and informative fields. Tennyson's *Idyls of the King* is cultural from both the poetic and historic standpoint. Kipling's virile verse is often read for pleasure by persons who normally avoid poetry and it is highly informative as well.

Expansion in the informative field adds both to pleasure and to culture. Through looking up facts, or reading supplementary material, or checking the opinions of different authors, you may advance far toward self-improvement by reading.

THE THIRD STEP: LEARNING

• *Learning,* the third step, has a twofold connotation. It applies not only to learning *from* reading, but to learning *what* to read. Here, the linkage between reading for pleasure, culture and information becomes very evident and almost automatic.

Through proper choice and expansion of reading, the elements of interest, attention and repetition merge into association, enabling you to remember quotations as well as facts. That constitutes learning *from* reading. The experience thus gained serves to pinpoint other material that will furnish further knowledge on a given subject. That is learning *what* to read.

THE FOURTH STEP: FINISHING

• *Finishing* what you need is the final step toward self-improvement. This is the biggest problem that confronts the modern reader, because of the great diversity of reading available today. It is very easy to lay aside a book and then forget it because a new reading interest intervenes.

This doesn't mean that you must grimly read every book from start to finish, ignoring all other reading for the time being.

That in itself is bad, as interest may wane during too sustained a reading period, and attention will accordingly lag, so that repetition becomes boring instead of helpful.

Obviously, then, it is unwise to take on too many reading projects at one time. This stresses the advantage of rapid reading, which enables you to finish one book before you start another. Often, you will find that when you read faster you remember more, because you get deeper into the subject as a whole while your mind is still fresh, and your reading intensity is also at a stronger pitch.

S-E-L-F Spells
Self-Improvement in Reading

The initial letters of these four steps: Selection, Expansion, Learning, Finishing, spell the word SELF which in its turn is the key to self-improvement. Thus the three initial types of reading—pleasure, cultural, informative—can be combined and implemented through the four steps described.

Demonstration of this is found through analysis of reading of the strictly "self-improvement" type, which has come strongly into vogue today. By comparison, where the writings of Benjamin Franklin were *recommended* for self-improvement, those of a modern writer like Dale Carnegie were *designed* for that purpose

Though the formula is similar, there is a difference between the old and the new. In his *Autobiography,* Franklin related his experiences in a way that aroused *interest.* He drew conclusions and comparisons that commanded *attention.* He summed them through reminders in the form of *repetition.* From these *associations,* readers gained the realization that the book was a guide to *self-improvement.*

In *How to Win Friends and Influence People,* Carnegie reveals his whole purpose before the reader reaches the opening paragraph, because the title tells it. But he immediately goes into anecdotes of personal experiences that carry *interest,* using them to draw *attention* to the purpose of each chapter which is driven home through *repetition.*

Advantages of Faster Reading

What has this to do with reading faster and remembering more? Just this: As you read, you can speed according to your need. With Franklin's story, you can move rapidly through much of the narration, watching for situations that promise philosophical observations, which can be noted in detail. In some of Carnegie's anecdotes, you can size up the situation in the opening paragraph and skim through to the nub in the last.

Always, you can return and "pick up" or "gather slack" as needed, so that nothing is lost through this effort toward speed. On the contrary, much may be gained. In going back, you will often know just where to look for something that you may have missed, due to some later reference that you encountered. That is better than dawdling too much along the way.

All this is based on two important points that apply to much of today's reading, especially the self-improvement type: Frequently, it has been given in *greater length than needed,* in some cases purposely overwritten, to see that nothing is missed; also, your aim in reading may be to get the *general idea,* rather than the by-products; or in some cases, you may be looking for certain *specific points* rather than the whole.

As a simple illustration, a reader picked up a book titled *Irons and Oxen* which had to do with superstitions and farming methods of the Roumanian peasants. This reader was interested only in superstitions. Hence, he could skim rapidly through the book, slowing only when he saw such references coming up.

In all book condensations, experienced editors go through the text, deleting according to the needs of the average reader. This works well for a mass audience, especially if the material itself is suited to such condensation, which it often is. On the other hand, an experienced reader can usually condense material himself, and if his reasons for reading a book differ from those of the average person, it is better that he should do so.

Special reading techniques have been designed for this purpose and are particularly suitable when applied to self-improvement.

Though similar, they vary in certain details, some being more elaborate than others. All are good, and in various ways combine elements of interest, attention and repetition with the all-inclusive factor of association, so valuable in reading to remember. They also incorporate the S-E-L-F steps that spell self-improvement.

Here are some of the most used techniques:

THE SPEED OR FIVE S METHOD

The letter S stands for Speed, which has five letters in all. In keeping with this, five more words beginning with an S are used to further the technique. In order, the procedure runs:

> SELECT your book and also select material from the table of contents to see if it interests you.
> SAMPLE some of the more likely material, or even a few random paragraphs to see if the style or treatment are satisfactory.
> SKIP to whatever portion of the book seems most desirable or worthy of immediate attention.
> SKIM through that portion—or the book as a whole—to acquire main ideas, without close reading.
> SCAN to strengthen those ideas and give closer attention to their details.

Some of these devices have already been alluded to in earlier chapters. With the Five S Technique, you are simply applying them in fuller measure. You do not have to follow the exact order given, nor do you have to use all five. What is more, their application may be variable, according to the book.

For example, if the book has a good index, you may do your selecting there. That, in turn, may provide you with several pointed samples. Your skipping, too, can be back and forth in the book, if you are working from an index.

Indiscriminate skipping is inadvisable where certain books are concerned. To skip through a story or a closely knit theme would be unwise. But with history, for example, you might want to know only about certain periods, so skipping to those would be quite justified on such occasions.

In skimming and scanning, you get deeper into the material and give it a more thorough reading if desired. One big advantage of the Five S Technique is that if you are already somewhat familiar with a subject, you can find out readily how much more a particular book has to offer.

It is good for comparing books, too. Anyone eager to learn about a subject can give half a dozen books the Five S treatment during a visit to a library and thereby choose the one that offers the best coverage.

THE RTP FORMULA

The letters RTP stand for Read The Problem, but they could also signify "*R*ound *T*ri*P*" because if properly applied, they will bring you right back to the starting point. An important advantage is that you will be better off if you happened to make a false start, which many readers do.

The RTP formula is particularly suited to explanatory or semi-technical material, especially if the reader is unfamiliar with it. For that reason, it enjoyed popularity with Army instructors who were anxious to get quick results with new trainees.

Time and again, a reader will skim through some statements and miss a few important ideas that are essential later on. Or he may speed his reading of a subject before he has it well in hand. By "reading the problem" and getting it thoroughly fixed in mind, little or no opportunity is left for false conclusions or wrong answers later on.

Applied to speed reading, the RTP formula means getting off to a slow but thorough start and pausing again when other important points crop up. Know where you stand before you start to speed.

THE PERU SYSTEM

This is a more extensive method of reading to remember. Again, a key-word, PERU, is made up of the initial letters of the stages in the process: Preview, Enquire, Read, Use.

This incorporates concepts already recommended, plus a further factor; namely Use.

• Your *Preview* is like a modified Five S Technique. You apply enough sampling, skimming or scanning to get an idea of the subject before tackling it.

• When you *Enquire,* you are using something of the RTP process. You go into the problem, if there is one, but in any event, you make sure of what you are after. Your preview helps, because you will be enquiring into certain facts of statements that you saw mentioned but did not necessarily understand.

• Next you *Read,* and the process can naturally be faster than usual, as you already have a working acquaintance with the subject and have looked into the material that is coming up. New facts fall in line like old acquaintances.

• You then *Use* the material thus acquired which is the final step of this formula and its main goal. With subjects that are fairly easy to learn or which are free from complex problems, this method is highly effective.

However, there are methods beyond PERU, most carefully designed as primary guides for use in the most demanding types of study, where accuracy is at a premium.

THE PQRST FORMULA

This is favored in higher brackets of instruction, as it contains the basic factors of the earlier formulas, but includes a few more that become essential in some forms of reading and study. The letters PQRST stand for Preview, Question, Read, State, Test, which are the five points of this system.

• *Preview,* as already defined, means noting the essential features of a book, as with other systems. This can be applied to whatever extent seems best, depending on the subject.

• *Question* is a noting of any problems or possible obstacles, which may require some reference work at the start. This is similar to RTP or an early stage of PERU.

• *Read* is the next and most comprehensive step, following the same pattern as with PERU. But instead of putting the acquired knowledge into immediate use, it is given more treatment.

• *State* what you have read. This may mean pausing after a chapter, or at any other stage. You must be sure of what you have read before you can use it. Not only that, you have one more stage.

• *Test* your newly acquired knowledge, either by self-examination or by having someone ask you questions on the subject. Once you can give the answers satisfactorily, the PQRST task is done.

SQ3R OR SURVEY Q3R

This is becoming perhaps the best known of all rapid reading techniques, particularly as a study discipline. It goes somewhat beyond the rest, though it is very similar to the PQRST formula.

In SQ3R, there are five steps: Survey, Question, and Three R's, consisting of Read, Recite, Review. These are handled as follows:

• *Survey* your material by studying chapter headings and looking for basic ideas. This is more definitive than a preview. The material may be surveyed almost to the outline stage.

• *Question* each point that you have surveyed, so that you have definite things to learn about. Don't just count on picking them up as you go along. Be ready for them.

• *Read* through the material which you have already covered twice before, so that surveying, questioning and reading have all been accomplished.

• *Recite* what you have thus learned. Note the strong forms of association that you have now brought into action. In reciting, your mind may go back to your survey, to a question, or to the actual reading. This linkage is a powerful memory factor.

• *Review* the whole subject, to make sure you have it right. If wrong or doubtful, check those points. Other reviews can follow at varied intervals.

Sometimes the term "Revise" is used instead of "Review,"

but it amounts to the same thing, as the purpose of a review is to check all details and if any are wrong, they must necessarily be revised.

Further Use of the Three R's.

Everyone is acquainted with the humorous reference to the Three R's of Learning: Reading, 'Riting and 'Rithmetic. As we have just seen, Reading also has three R's—including itself as one—in the forms of Read, Recite, Review.

These have long been used in their own right, as the basic factors of memory. Moreover, to *read* requires *interest;* to *recite* demands *attention;* to *review* involves *repetition.* Accordingly, if you have a subject all selected and a clear path in mind as to its study, you can often read, recite and review without any further preliminaries.

This is the process used in memorizing poetry or a speech, hence it can be applied broadly whenever you read to remember. In word-for-word memorization—as with poetry—stress is on the latter stages. On the other hand, with regular reading, where you seek to remember general ideas or various facts that do not have to be stated in exact form, the emphasis is on the reading itself. But you must be sure that the other R's follow.

The techniques just given all work to that end, namely, providing patterns for efficiency in reading to remember. They should be used when appropriate, and to whatever degree may be required. However, there are other ways to go about remembering, systems whereby special facts may be pegged, often with an incredible degree of permanence. Those ways are known as artificial memory systems, and they can be applied to daily reading with remarkable results. That will be the subject of the next chapter.

Memory
devices
as standbys
in
VIII   remembering
reading

In order to make your resources as to reading techniques more complete, you will now be given a working acquaintance with general memory devices and their exploitation in reading. These start with simple mnemonic aids, and also introduce key-words of the acrostic and acronym types.

The very points that you have considered in speeding and improving your reading, reveal themselves as memory tabs which can be expanded and elaborated as you proceed.

After distinguishing between reading techniques and study methods, you enter the field that is applicable to both; that of actual memory systems, stemming from ancient methods into modern devices.

Memory Systems which
Really Work Wonders

• *The Room System,* a basic "topical" memory aid, is described, with a special illustration. How this is applied to recalling historical accounts, and in the memorizing of poetry, are included here.

• *The Chain System* is given as an alternate method, with representative material that can be readily memorized and tested while you read.

The twin aims of reading faster and remembering more have a firm common ground that can be summed in the single word *association*. This begins with recognition of the alphabet and the simplest of word formations; and it carries right on through to the memorization of formulas for self-improvement and their utilization, as described in the previous chapter.

Now we come to the application of *artificial* devices as aids in remembering material that you have just read. Actually, any efforts to intensify interest, add to attention, or renew repetition, are all aids to association, and are among those which have been presented throughout this book. To a large degree, however, such efforts may be classed as strictly *natural* aids.

The reading techniques given in the previous chapter are designed to speed reading and increase memorization through natural processes, but they approach the status of artificial aids. Their names, the Five S Method, the RTP and PERU systems, as well as such formulas as PQRST and SQ3R, are all memory joggers.

You can prove that to your own satisfaction right now, by pausing and trying to recall the meanings of the letters in each case. If you can, you have taken advantage of a time honored memory device, the use of simple mnemonics, or word symbols formed by initials or parts of longer words comprising a word group or series. Simple initials or coined words also come into this category. They generally have a catchy significance, and are called acronyms when applied to a compound term.

Thus, the initials PERU, as used to define a reading technique are a simple mnemonic since they have the pronunciation of an actual word, "PERU." On the other hand, the simple mnemonic PQRST, being only a string of initials, resembles an acronym, with the letters occurring in alphabetical order. In the case of SQ3R, a catchy acronym type word is provided so as to easily remember that reading technique.

Applying Acronyms
as Memory Devices

Coined words, such as Nabisco for National Biscuit Company or Necco, for New England Confectionary Company, date well back, along with such explosive expressions as TNT for trinitro-toluene. But those were oddities or comparative rarities in their time, whereas the use of acronyms has now become very common, and sometimes the titles themselves are coined to fit the acronym.

Thus, today we have such understandable acronyms as UN for United Nations, Interpol for International Police Commission, CORE for Committee on Racial Equality, AID for Agency for International Development, CAB for Civil Aeronautics Board, Delmarva for the peninsula composed of parts of Delaware (Del), Maryland (Mar) and Virginia (Va), along with a great host of others.

Even when such acronyms take over as actual words, it is easy to link them to the full meaning of the word combinations that they represent. This raises the question: When possible, why not apply acronyms as memory devices by making up new ones as you read, thus pegging essential facts and retaining them in mind?

The answer is, you can, though actually and in all likelihood, you may be using coined words rather than true acronyms. The difference is that a coined word need have no direct link with the idea that it represents, other than your own association. That, however, may be enough to fulfill its purpose for you. A coined word, properly applied, can serve as an acronym where an individual is concerned, and it may also come into general usage as a memory jog.

Examples of Effective
Simple Mnemonics

One excellent example is the memorizing of the names of the Great Lakes. Most persons learn them in the order of size:

Superior, Huron, Michigan, Erie, Ontario. Later, in recalling them, somebody might miss one name, or even forget the exact number. People have much to remember today, beside the names of the Great Lakes. If they should miss one, almost any hint will bring it to mind.

For this purpose, the simple mnemonic HOMES is used. It is easy to remember, because today the *Great Lakes* are surrounded by *Homes*. The initial letters in the key-word HOMES stand for Huron, Ontario, Michigan, Erie, Superior. You will never forget the names of the Great Lakes if you peg them by the code word HOMES.

As another example: For the states on the Pacific Coast, you think of A COW. The initial letters are Alaska (A)—California (C) —Oregon (O)—Washington (W). The cow starts from Alaska and jumps clear down to California, which should be easy, considering that a cow once jumped over the moon. Then it works its way back through Oregon to Washington.

If you are reading British history, with all the problems that it encountered following the Norman Conquest, you will be WISE if you remember—and being wise, how can you forget it?—that there are four important nationalities involved in the recurrent conflicts: Welsh, Irish, Scotch, English. Their initials spell WISE.

Such memory jogs can sometimes be arranged for emphasis in the style of acrostics, with the capital letters forming a vertical key-word, the components being horizontal, as:

Huron	Alaska	Wales
Ontario		Ireland
Michigan	Cow	Scotland
Erie	Oregon	England
Superior	Washington	

The limitation of the simple mnemonic, acronym, or the acrostic lies in the fact that comparatively few formations are readily possible. Some word groups do not lend themselves to this treatment. However, when applied to reading to remember, this limitation can often be overcome.

Use of the Simple Mnemonic
in Remembering an Entire Article

When reading to remember, you start reading with a reading technique, where the material is concerned. In the simpler cases, the RTP method may suffice, or you may give the subject matter a rapid PERU treatment.

As an example, consider an article on *The Importance of Ideas in Modern Life:*

The writer begins with the premise that ingenuity is essential to ideas and their formation, but that today people have to be ingenious in order to keep pace with the world around them. Examples of such ingenuity are then given.

Because you possess this latent ability, the proper step is to develop it. There are many ways in which this can be done individually, and these are described, all representing challenges of everyday life.

Since other persons are confronted with the same problems, you should exchange ideas with them, either directly or indirectly, by reading up on other people's experiences and their advice on handling situations.

Having prepared yourself, application of ideas is essential. Anything learned should be applied, otherwise it is more apt to be lost. Through application, you learn at first hand if an idea is worth while. If it isn't, further measures are needed.

Simplification then becomes the final step. Almost all the great ideas in this complex world are the result of many minds, each working to simplify our current problem. Make that your goal and watch how opportunities come your way!

The paragraphs given above represent the substance of the

article, which might run from half a dozen pages, perhaps up to a booklet of five chapters, according to the author's treatment. If a short article, you could "read the problem" with each paragraph, using the RTP process to fix each point in mind. With a longer article, or one which might require feeling your way, it would be better to "preview" and "enquire"—the first two steps in PERU—before beginning to "read" in detail.

In either case, you would seek a suitable key-word tying in each phase with the main theme. Now, the main theme, as stated in the title, can be summed up in the word IDEAS. That becomes your simple mnemonic. What you need is a series of keys, stemming from those initial letters in the style of an acrostic.

Going through the five paragraphs, you find that the first deals with *ingenuity* as a necessary ability. The second paragraph stresses *development*. The *exchange* of ideas is recommended in the third paragraph. The fourth points up *application* as a necessary phase. In *simplification,* we have the fifth and final key.

Tabulate those in order as if they were chapter headings and you have:

Ingenuity	the basic factor
Development	improving that ability
Exchange	acquiring new methods
Application	putting these to use
Simplicity	the ultimate result

Note that the initial letters of your "keys" spell the theme word: IDEAS. From then on, if you want to recall that author's views on the subject of "Ideas," just take your mnemonic, IDEAS and spell it out I-D-E-A-S. The keys of Ingenuity, Development, Exchange, Application, Simplicity will fall in line. More than mere keys, they can be regarded as letters in a combination, each providing associations of its own from which much of the entire article can be recalled.

Suggested Variations
in Acrostic Components

The example given was specially chosen because it fitted so well with the acrostic device. In fact, writers occasionally provide keys for that purpose. But when keys are lacking, it is often possible to provide your own, though it may be necessary to use equivalents rather than the more obvious keys, in order to form your mnemonic.

In *The Importance of Ideas in Modern Life,* the first paragraph applies to *invention* as much as *ingenuity.* The *development* of ideas requires observance of *detail.* Along with the *exchange* of ideas, you gain *experience.* To be properly *applied* an idea must be *adaptable* to use. Through *simplification,* you achieve *success.*

Then, in place of the stated keys, you can use their counterparts, or suggested keys, and still spell out I-D-E-A-S:

Invention	which requires	*Ingenuity*
Detail	as a sure process of	*Development*
Experience	as the result of	*Exchange*
Adaptability	gained through	*Application*
Success	as the outcome of	*Simplification*

In cases where stated keys are satisfactory, suggested keys are not needed, though with certain persons, they may prove preferable as memory jogs. For instance, *invention* might be more suitable than *ingenuity.* That is a matter of individual choice. Still, where the keys won't fall into line, or are vague in themselves, equivalents come into their own.

Turning Ideas Into
Suitable Equivalents

Here is an excellent case in point, taken from an article on style, as used in speech and writing, dealing with the phase of "Force," along with a list of rules. It runs:

Force is required to produce an effect on the mind of the hearer. He must not only understand what we have to say, but have some emotion in regard to it; else he will have forgotten our words before we have fairly uttered them. Force is the appeal that words make to the feeling, as clearness is the appeal they make to the understanding.

The thing that most of us wish to find out is, how to write with force. Force is attained in various ways, summarized as follows:

1. By using words which are in themselves expressive.
2. By placing those words in emphatic positions in the sentence.
3. By varying the form and length of successive sentences so that the reader or hearer shall never be worried by monotony.
4. By figures of speech, or constant comparison and illustration, and making words suggest ten times as much as they say.
5. By keeping persistently at one idea, though from every possible point of view, and without repetition of any kind, until that idea has sunk into the mind of the hearer and has been fully comprehended.

Analyzing the above, we find it suited to an acrostic style memory device because the writer has discussed FORCE in terms of five rules, and the word itself contains that many letters. On the other hand, there is very little in the way of keys to the word "Force," so you must form your own equivalents.

Looking through the first paragraph, you will find the word "feeling," which is the mood of the reader or listener, to which force makes its appeal. Conveniently, feeling can become the first rule.

This establishes the reader's standpoint, so if words are put in emphatic positions, they will come under immediate *observation* on the reader's part, setting the second rule.

The third rule concerns *readability,* which can be taken as a key. The fourth already has a key in the word comparison. For the fifth, *emphasis* is a good inclusive term, though *expression* would also do. One dictionary definition for "emphasis" is "special impressiveness of expression" so that gives *emphasis* strong choice.

Spell them out, as just given, adding an appropriate sidelight to each, and you have:

Feeling	aroused through expressive words.
Observation	based on placement of such words.
Readability	through variance in sentence form.
Comparison	by figurative and illustrative suggestions.
Emphasis	on one idea from all possible viewpoints.

In spelling out the major phases of a theme through the use of words in acrostic style, it is not always necessary to keep them in exact order. That was illustrated similarly with the mnemonic HOMES as a mental tab for the names of the Great Lakes. Their size, or geographical position did not matter; or more correctly, those points could be considered once the names were properly pegged.

Also, in using initials to form a simple mnemonic, there is often choice of the theme word itself. Suppose you were reading an article on *The Place of America in Modern History* and you found that it could be subdivided into seven phases. For your mnemonic you could use either AMERICA or HISTORY, whichever offered the best list of initial letters in forming the words for a suitable acrostic style arrangement.

As a memory aid, the acrostic plan is limited in scope and therefore should be applied only when its use is natural and easy. Sometimes subject headings fall into line; on other occasions, it is simple to coin them. In situations when they become strained or too far-fetched, it is better to use some other memory device. This will become evident, as you note the devices that follow. Your know-how is then applied to choosing the type most suited to the existing need.

Distinguishing Between Reading Techniques and Study Methods

All general reading techniques of the types so far given, can by natural extension be converted into study methods. The emphasis on study becomes greater according to the increased complexity of the system. Thus the RTP formula, by its very admonition, "Read the Problem," stresses *reading* as its aim; whereas the SQ3R formula with its five different stages, plainly predicts that some degree of study may be involved, and that it can be elaborated as required.

When you *read to remember,* you undergo a *learning process,* which also occurs in *systematic study.* Hence it is difficult to draw a line of demarcation between intensive reading and applied study. In a sense, there is no division; one simply blends into the other, because your motivation is self-improvement, whether cultural, social, commercial, scientific, or a medley of such purposes.

However, for broad discussion, we can class all reading techniques as extensions of the natural reading process, with the addition of every improvement and other measures applicable to speed and fuller comprehension; whereas, a study system, purely as such, could vary its reading speeds and techniques and at times get away from reading entirely. In short:

In reading techniques, we learn by reading to remember.

In study methods, we learn by remembering what we read.

There are times when the two procedures are practically identical, especially in simpler forms. But when they diverge—and they can do so in the simpler stages as well as the complex—their common target, that of memorization, gains a special significance and requires separate modes of treatment.

Linking Reading to Remembering

Memorization involves notations, which may be either mental or written. In reading, mental notes are more logical. Even in heavy or important reading, use of an advanced formula like the SQ3R allows for a review, bringing up those mental notes as you come to the material involved.

Such a review is a double test: You find out how well you remember your notations; you also can decide if some points were worth noting at all. The upshot is a series of mental pegs, which may already be firmly fixed. If not, some measure must be taken to drive them home. That is where an artificial memory device can be used to great advantage.

As an example: In literary composition, there are three basic requirements: Unity, Coherence and Emphasis. Each is so important that it practically becomes a subject in itself. During any discussion of literature, they will crop up repeatedly, so there is no need to "code" them by some "key" or slogan. Just remember them as they are: Unity, Coherence, Emphasis, depending on repetition to keep them in mind.

The same would apply to Faith, Hope and Charity, or the famous Triumvirate of Caesar, Pompey and Crassus, as well as many other cases. In contrast, to remember that the British Colonies of Bahamas, Barbados and Bermuda once had identical forms of government, they can be mentally tabbed as the "Three B's." As another example, the old Cleveland, Cincinnati, Chicago and St. Louis Railroad was nicknamed "The Big Four" because its terminal cities were at that time the four largest in the Midwest.

The use of simple mnemonics, acronyms, or acrostics as memory tabs has already been discussed, and again it should be stressed that this is valuable when it becomes an adjunct or extension of the reading technique. But if you must stop and either strain or begin all over to form a "key" list, it is better to turn to some other device.

Otherwise, you will be sacrificing the speed of reading technique for the slowness of the full-fledged study system. Where the reader lists things mentally—at least for a start—the student makes written notations. He may even plod with some of these, writing them out at length, figuring that he can fill in on other facts later. Just as the reader may forego a few unneeded mental pegs when he comes to review them, so can the student cross out his surplus notes or reduce them in size, when he writes out his final list.

Now, it is quite all right for a reader to make written notes too, provided he does not slow his reading process or interfere with his reading technique. Often, the brief pause needed to weigh a fact, or consider an important statement word by word, will allow time to write a word or phrase, instead of merely repeating it mentally. A reader may also mark words or paragraphs as he proceeds, in order to speed his review with such techniques as the PQRST or SQ3R. When doing so, he should regard it as part of the reading process, which is 100 per cent mental. His notes in some instances may play about the same role in his reading as his doodles might in the course of a telephone conversation.

If he winds up with whole pages of notes that require special consideration of their own, he is not reading to remember. He is reading to study. He will have to study those notes to remember what he read, which means an additional process. This defeats the speed factor, which is the prime mover of every reading technique. It would have been better to start with a study system and follow it throughout, making reading secondary or subordinate.

That is why the more elaborate techniques have come to be regarded as study systems. There is no need for going to such extremes in general reading on a subject. Study can come later, if and when required. Overloading with unnecessary notes simply means piling up more things to remember instead of pegging those that really count.

You are confronted with the all-important factor of remembering the material thus gained. You can usually do that just as well while reading—as with the RTP technique—or while reviewing—as with SQ3R—as you can after a study session requiring copious notes. In fact, the printed reading material is often easier to peg than the written notes that emerge from sustained study.

Any time memorization goes beyond the self-sustaining stage—as with such essential factors as "Unity, Coherence, Emphasis" and others of that type—you may want to utilize an artificial memory device and peg the needed items. From there, you go right on with your reading to the finish. If a lot of such pegs are needed, or any should be stronger, you can check them during your review.

All this becomes part of the reading technique itself—or an

extension thereof—provided the right device is used. A good plan is to test each device in ordinary reading, thus gaining familiarity with its use, so it can be employed as needed.

The simple mnemonic, acronym and acrostic type devices have been detailed, and may be used when suitable. Any chance "dodges" are also helpful, like the "Three B's" mentioned earlier. However, all so far described have obvious limitations. Getting on to those with broader scope, we turn to:

THE ROOM SYSTEM
(*Simple Topical Device*)

This is the oldest of artifical aids for extensive memorization. In a sense it is the progenitor of all that have followed. Its popularity goes back to an ancient Greek poet named Simonides, who lived about the year 470 B.C., and discovered its effectiveness by accident.

Simonides attended a dinner where he recited some of his verses and shortly after he left, the roof fell in, crushing all the diners. After the debris was cleared away, Simonides was able to identify the victims because he could recall the exact place where each man had been.

This impressed Simonides with the fact that objects might be remembered by visualizing them in certain places, so he developed a memory system along that line. It eventually reached Rome, where it was used by Cicero, the most famous of Roman orators, in preparing speeches, which he memorized by that method.

Cicero at first moved about from room to room, or patio to garden, as he recited each new portion of his speech. Then by simply recalling the floor plan of his house, the individual subjects sprang instantly to his mind. Objects could be remembered in the same way by allotting them mentally to the imaginary floor plan and this could be elaborated by subdividing each room and visualizing objects in different spots around it. The mental tour could then be continued to another room, and so on.

With the decline of the Roman Empire, the science of mnemonics, or artificial memory as it has been called, was preserved in manuscripts and nurtured in monasteries. Among the early manuscripts devoted to the art of memory and referred to by later authorities, was one written by Roger Bacon, a famous English friar who was born in the year 1214.

Then, in 1491, the year before Columbus sailed for America, mnemonics received a distinct impetus through a book by Petrus Ravennas, who was among the first memory experts to give public exhibitions, which won him acclaim throughout Italy. He became known as Petrus a Memoria, and was even lauded as the discoverer of a new art.

Other experts' books had appeared and continued to be published at intervals, all apparently basing their work on the methods of the ancients, often with modifications and improvements. An article by a man named Johann Winkelmann has been cited as ushering in the modern era of mnemonics. He utilized the topical system of the ancients, but also claimed to be possessor of a "most fertile secret" where memory was concerned. This was revealed to scholars of his day in a 1648 periodical printed in Latin. Winkelmann's secret was his version of an early form of the figure alphabet, which has become the most highly developed of all mnemonic methods.

However, the original system exploited by Simonides is quite as good as ever. In this modern era, with so many new things to remember, it can be even more useful than in ancient times. You can readily try out the "room system" for yourself. Just picture yourself in a room of your choice, with its familiar furnishings: then visualize objects in a set rotation. Later you will be surprised how easily you recall them through such associations.

Putting the Room System into Practice

Suppose that you choose a living room as a base for your mnemonic operation and that it is arranged as follows. As you enter, beginning at your left, there is a telephone table; then a couch; next, a TV set in the far left corner. In the wall opposite you, there is a fireplace; in the corner to the right of that, a writing desk. In the side wall at the right, there is a large picture window; in the near right corner there is a book-case; then comes a big easy chair.

That makes eight "places" or "locations", and it should prove easy to remember eight other objects or items, by simply visualizing them in those spots. That is the way the topical system is frequently used, in remembering shopping lists and the like. It is a surprising device, because the more ridiculous or incongruous the combined pictures, the stronger they become.

Returning to our purpose of *reading to remember,* we will apply the system of places much as Cicero did in reciting his orations; but in this case, each link will involve a paragraph from a printed page.

Where can we locate a suitable subject told in eight paragraphs? Just glance back and you will find it in our brief survey of the subject of the "Room System" itself.

Here is the procedure:

- *Paragraph 1:*   *Location:*   Telephone table.
  On the table is a life-sized bust of Simonides, the famous Greek poet, bearing the statement: Simonides, 470 B.C.
- *Paragraph 2:*   *Location:*   The couch.
  The ceiling has fallen in, or can still be collapsing, so that the couch is buried in the wreckage.
- *Paragraph 3:*   *Location:*   The TV set.
  Who is talking away on the TV, but Cicero in person, addressing the crowd in the Roman forum.
- *Paragraph 4:*   *Location:*   The fireplace.
  Stooped beside the fireplace are two ancient Romans studying a mammoth floor plan by the firelight.
- *Paragraph 5:*   *Location:*   The writing desk.

On the writing desk, ready for serving, is a nice big plate of bacon signifying Roger Bacon.

- *Paragraph ,6:   Location: The picture window.*
There, Christopher Columbus is shaking hands with Petrus Ravennas. Columbus came from Genoa, and there is a city named Ravenna straight across the Italian peninsula from Genoa. All that links in a fanciful picture of Ravennas wishing Columbus lots of luck next year.

- *Paragraph 7:   Location: The bookcase.*
Winkelmann peering over the bookcase and giving us the wink (for Winkelmann) because he has a secret, which can be in a little pamphlet that he is showing us.

- *Paragraph 8:   Location: The easy chair.*
You are seated in the easy chair, looking around the room and noting the things just mentioned in the rotation given.

This illustration shows how adaptable the "Room System" is for certain types of reading. It goes well with informative material that is stronger on descriptions than on mere statistics. In the sample given, only eight "room objects" were included, as no additional ones were needed. The more usual plan is to have ten. Thus there could be a mirror and a straight chair on the near side of the easy chair, making ten in all.

If you need to remember more than ten items, you go into another familiar room and proceed from there. According to one tradition, the old Romans carried this system to such lengths that they created one "mental" building after another, until they had whole cities of them.

Cicero used each mental image as a "key" for a topic of his speech. In reading, you can do practically the same. Naturally, details must be clustered about the "target" image. In view of the fact that the keys are solid and in order of discussion, it is easier.

The greater consequence, however, is this:

If, as you read, you were ready with your "places" for the

"items" that you visualized, your reading process would not take too much longer than normally without their use. Yet, with practice, you could finish by remembering almost all that is pertinent in what you had read!

Will the "Room System" function that way always?

Yes, always, if what you read fits into your room. However, it doesn't always do that. In that case, you must broaden your scope, or better still, let the material itself set the scene.

Further Extension
of the Topical Device

Take this example of the first inauguration of George Washington as President of the United States, on April 30, 1789, in a description by Washington Irving:

> At twelve o'clock, the city troops paraded before Washington's door, and soon after the committees of Congress and heads of departments came in their carriages. At half-past twelve the procession moved forward preceded by the troops; next came the committees and heads of departments in their carriages; then Washington in a coach of state. The foreign ministers and a long train of citizens brought up the rear.
>
> Before reaching the hall, Washington and his suite alighted from their carriages and passed through the troops, who were drawn up on each side, into the hall and Senate chamber, where the Vice-president, the Senate, and House of Representatives were assembled. The Vice-president, John Adams, recently inaugurated, advanced and conducted Washington to a chair of state at the upper end of the room. A solemn silence prevailed when the Vice-president rose and informed him that all things were prepared for him to take the oath of office required by the Constitution.
>
> The oath was to be administered by the chancellor of the State of New York in a balcony in front of the Senate chamber, and in full view of an immense multitude occupying the street, the windows and even roofs of the adjacent houses. The balcony formed a kind of open recess, with lofty columns supporting the roof. In the center was a table with a covering of crimson velvet, upon which lay a superbly bound Bible on a crimson velvet cushion. This was all the paraphernalia that had been provided for this august scene.
>
> All eyes were fixed upon the balcony when at the appointed hour, Washington made his appearance accompanied by various public

functionaries. He was clad in a full suit of dark-brown cloth of American manufacture, with a steel-hilted dress-sword, white silk stockings and silver shoe-buckles. His hair was dressed and powdered in the fashion of the day, and worn in a bag and solitaire.

His entrance on the balcony was hailed by universal shouts. He was evidently moved by this demonstration of public affection. Advancing to the front of the balcony he laid his hand upon his heart, bowed several times and then retreated to an arm-chair near the table. The populace seemed to understand that the scene had overcome him, and were hushed into profound silence.

After a few moments Washington rose and again came forward. John Adams, the Vice-president, stood on his right; on his left, the chancellor of the state, Robert R. Livingston; in the rear were others. The chancellor advanced to administer the oath prescribed by the Constitution, and Mr. Otis, the secretary of the senate, held up the Bible on its crimson cushion. The oath was read slowly and distinctly, Washington at the same time laying his hand on the open Bible. When it was concluded, he replied solemnly, "I swear—so help me, God!" Mr. Otis would have raised the Bible to his lips, but he bowed down reverently and kissed it.

The chancellor now stepped forward, waved his hand and exclaimed, "Long live George Washington, President of the United States!" At this moment, a flag was displayed on the cupola of the hall; on which signal, there was a general discharge of artillery on the Battery. All the bells in the city rang out a joyful peal, and the multitude rent the air with acclamations.

Washington again bowed to the people and returned into the Senate chamber, where he delivered to both houses his inaugural address, characterized by his usual modesty, moderation and good sense, but uttered with a voice deep, slightly tremulous and so low as to demand close attention in the listeners.

He then proceeded with the assemblage to St. Paul's church, where prayers were read by Dr. Prevost, Bishop of the Protestant Episcopal Church in New York, who had been appointed by the Senate one of the chaplains of Congress. So closed the ceremonies of the inauguration.

In reading the above with intention of remembering its more important details, the two points mentioned become obvious; namely that the scenes are too large for "room" placement, and that they set their own logical locale, in rotation. Accordingly, as you read, you set those scenes in sequence; or if you skim or give the material a preview, you pick your "places" then, and form the mental pictures as you read.

Since these pictures deal with actualities, you will do better to dwell on details, rather than introduce grotesque or distorted images as memory joggers. Action, color, anything vivid, can be used to strengthen the associations. Pick your "places" just as you would in your own room, somewhat as follows:

- *Place 1*: *The Parade* (Paragraph 1)
  Picture the procession leaving Washington's door as described, establishing the pattern for future inaugural parades.
- *Place 2*: *The Reception* (Paragraph 2)
  Arrival at Federal Hall in New York, with Washington entering doorway and proceeding to Senate chamber.
- *Place 3*: *The Balcony* (Paragraphs 3 & 4)
  Since the third paragraph is largely a description of the balcony, it simply sets the place more exactly and the fourth paragraph links Washington with it.
- *Place 4*: *The Crowd* (Paragraphs 5 & 6)
  Again, two paragraphs combine effectively, because the scene is described as if viewed by someone below. The crowd's reaction, the silence, the dramatic action on the balcony, all would have been noted by an onlooker.
- *Place 5*: *The Panorama* (Paragraph 7)
  Here, moving back from the vantage spot of the well-placed spectator, we gain an overall picture from the outskirts; balcony, flag, artillery, bells—all included in the graphic scene.
- *Place 6*: *The Senate Chamber* (Paragraph 8)
  The natural sequence of the inaugural address, as delivered on that occasion.
- *Place 7*: *The Church* (Paragraph 9)
  The arrival there, with conclusion of ceremonies.

Once you have formed those associations, you can fill in on details to any extent desired. The sequence will remain set, enabling you to recall the description from beginning to end. Any chance lapse, as forgetting Place 6 (the Senate Chamber) will be jogged into your mind by the continuity itself.

You can apply the same rules to other descriptions and narrations, fitting them to your "places" or to their own, as is best suited to each case. The fact that distorted images or ridiculous scenes were not needed as association strengtheners in the "Washington Inaugural" does not rule them out of other historical accounts.

Varied Forms
of "Picture Placement"

In reading about the Battle of Waterloo, you might picture Wellington as tall, thin, almost a human bean-pole in contrast to Napoleon, whose short, portly stature could be given dwarfish, roly-poly proportions. Caricature is always an effective device where memory is concerned, but it should not be introduced to the detriment of other essential factors.

Just as the Ancient Romans built "mental" cities for their topical memory aids, so can you extend your scope of "places." Instead of a room, you can take a mental trip by car, leaving the garage, going down a drive, stopping for gas, going onto the Freeway, approaching an underpass, and so on. Or you can imagine yourself entering an air terminal, buying a ticket, taking off, flying over the ocean, arriving in Paris, or whatever else will provide "places" to serve as mental pegs for whatever you read to remember.

The Topical Device works especially well in memorization of poetry. As an example, one student learned *The Landing of The Pilgrims* by imagining himself moving about a college campus, to a new place for each stanza. He saw "breaking waves dash high" on a porch where he pictured himself standing. The "heavy night hung dark" over a lawn where he went next. "The true-hearted came" to a playground wearing true blue hearts emblazoned on their jackets. All other essentials of the poem were given appropriate mental tabs.

Going to the other extreme, there are poems which set their own "places" for memorization, or can be linked with some unique device. A good example is *Sheridan's Ride,* in which General Sheridan raced "from Winchester, twenty miles away" to turn the tide of a Civil War battle. Stanzas bring him to "fifteen miles," then "ten miles," and then "five miles away," each distance being a memory marker. That poem could be tied in nicely with a modern road map.

In the "Washington Inaugural" account, one scene tended to link with the next. Such links should be noted as memory jogs. They are good with poetry, where you might skip a stanza, or any reading where you might miss an important paragraph. On occasion, such links can be used as memory devices in their own right, where other methods may prove difficult. This is called:

THE CHAIN SYSTEM

Years ago, a cartoonist made up a daily panel entitled "Opportunity Knocks But Once," showing quaint situations where someone took advantage of a lucky circumstance. The prize job of the series was the following picture:

There was one tiny hole near the center of a courtyard. Making for that hole was a wriggling worm, which was almost there. Just behind the worm was a swooping bird, its beak open to gulp the squirmy morsel. Behind the bird, a small boy was swinging a net downward intent on snaring the bird. Behind the boy, a man with a badge saying "Truant Officer" was about to clamp a hand on the boy's shoulder.

Here are four distinct links to a chain:

1. Hole and worm. 2. Worm and bird. 3. Bird and boy. 4. Boy and officer.

Think of the first and it carries you to the second; that in turn suggests the third link, which leads into the fourth. All five items fall in line: Hole, worm, bird, boy, officer.

Putting the Chain System
into Practice

Now, let us test this Chain System as an artificial memory
device with an article entitled *Along Newfoundland and Labrador*:

The most northerly lighthouse on the coast of the American con-
tinent stands at Belle Isle, at the head of the straits of that name,
northeast of Newfoundland. By what freak it was called Belle Isle,
I cannot say; for even the old navigators had such a horror of it that
on their charts they marked it with a figure of a demon.

As the little mail-steamer plunged and rolled past it through the
surge, the rugged mass of rock crouched there as if ready to seize
its prey of ships and human lives. The surf flashed around its base
like a long row of glistening teeth. A huge iceberg had drifted in and
lay stranded at one end of the island; far up on the rocks was the
lighthouse; on a shelf below stood a little hut with provisions for ship-
wrecked sailors; the gray morning mists made the sea look heavy and
sodden, and altogether this glimpse of Belle Isle was the most desolate
scene I had ever beheld.

Over our bow the barren coast of Labrador was faintly outlined, and
as the lighthouse dropped astern, I felt that we were indeed drawing
away from civilization; and this feeling was strengthened when, as
we turned our prow northward, we sighted the vanguard of the seemingly endless procession of huge icebergs drifting slowly down in single
file from the mysterious regions of the north.

We had met with single bergs along the Newfoundland coast, but
off Labrador they became a constant and grand feature in the sea-
ward sky. I doubt if they can be seen anywhere else in such numbers,
variety and grandeur. The branch of the Gulf Stream which pushes its
way into the Arctic Ocean has sufficient force left when it is deflected
by the frozen boundary of that sea to send an icy current down the
Labrador coast. One morning, when I went up on deck, I counted no
less than one hundred and thirty-five huge ones. Some were great
solid blocks of ice; others were arched with numerous Gothic passage-
ways; some reached with spire-like grace high up into the air; all
reflected with prismatic glory the rays of the sun.

The "iron-bound" coast of Labrador is guarded by groups of islands
—barren, hopeless, and forlorn looking rocks, all the more desolate in
appearance for the miserable fishing huts or "tilts" which have been
thrown together on them. Entering through some narrow passage,
between these islands, the steamer anchors for the night in a rock-
bound basin; for it is too dangerous work to navigate the Labrador
waters after dark.

The narrow passages are called "tickles" and aptly so, for it seems as if the sea had reached out foamy fingers and tickled the rocky ribs of the coast until it split its sides with grim, stormy laughter. One evening we found one of these tickles nearly blocked by a huge iceberg that had drifted into it and grounded. We passed near enough to feel its chilling breath, and to have thrown a biscuit on it, as the sailors say.

We had hardly anchored in the harbor before we heard loud reports in rapid succession, like the firing of field artillery. Looking in the direction from which they came, we saw above the heights that surrounded the basin, the peak of the iceberg swaying slowly and majestically to and fro, and finally disappearing, a peak of different shape rising up from behind the height and taking its place. Possibly the wash from our steamer had disturbed the iceberg's equilibrium.

I think that the height of icebergs is usually overstated. When an object towers above you, it is apt to seem much higher than it really is. At first sight, I thought some of the bergs we passed were four or five hundred feet high, but I doubt if the highest was over two hundred. But you can imagine what a vast mass of ice a berg is, when I remind you that only about one tenth of it is above water.

It is dangerous to venture near an iceberg, because you never know when you may strike upon its submerged portion as upon a rock. Of course some icebergs are mere mounds, and the fishermen have a cheerful method of securing their ice-supply by going out in their boats, catching a small berg and towing it ashore.

Forging the Links in the Chain

Now, to forge the links in the memory chain as suggested by the above description:

- *Link A*: Paragraphs 1 & 2:
  Paragraph 1 tells of Belle Isle being shown on charts as a demon, which links with its crouching mass described in Paragraph 2. So think of it as a real live demon.
- *Link B*: Paragraphs 2 & 3.
  The demon's surfy teeth snare icebergs and ships—as indicated by the hut in Paragraph 2—so the picture link shows our ship shying away from that, as in Paragraph 3.
- *Link C*: Paragraphs 3 & 4.
  We are headed northward in Paragraph 3, so our picture

links show bigger, grander icebergs and more of them, in Paragraph 4. Visualize the procession.

- *Link D*:   Paragraph 4 & 5.
  The link here is the Gulf Stream carrying the bergs toward the coast of Labrador in Paragraph 4, which is protected by its iron-bound islands as specified in Paragraph 5.
- *Link E*:   Paragraphs 5 & 6.
  Getting to shelter behind those islands is necessary, according to Paragraph 5 and it can be ticklish business, linking with the term "tickles" applied to the channels in Paragraph 6.
- *Link F*:   Paragraphs 6 & 7.
  The link here is the double chill, first provided by the chilling breath of the iceberg in Paragraph 6, and followed by the chilling sound like field artillery in Paragraph 7.
- *Link G*:   Watching the iceberg change peaks in Paragraph 7, allows opportunity to gauge its height as less than imagined, linking with the estimates in Paragraph 8.
- *Link H*:   Paragraphs 8 & 9
  The fact that nine-tenths of an iceberg is below the surface, as described in Paragraph 8, links with the danger of running aground on one, as stated in Paragraph 9. The danger is less, of course, with a small berg.

The Chain System Summarized

In forming links, choose those best suited to your imagination or picturization. Make sure that you have the full gist of each paragraph, and if need be, look for minor details that can be incorporated into the picture links. In some cases, less links are required. If the material is self-evident, it forms its own chain without the need of artificial memory aids. Then, picture links become necessary only to hook up occasional ideas that would otherwise be dissociated.

A good test for the Chain System is to read two similar articles, or two parts of the same article, at about the same speed.

But in one case, read it for substance alone; with the other, utilize the memory chain. Afterward, see how much you remember of each. You may be surprised by the added efficacy of the Chain System.

Other special memory aiding devices suited to reading and remembering will be detailed in the next chapter.

Using

picture

systems

for

IX   more effective

retention

Continuing your introduction to artificial memory devices, you will now become acquainted with one that has been most highly developed, the Figure Alphabet or Phonetic Numeral Code. It is given here with a series of ten "keys" which aid in rapid "pegging" of items that would otherwise be hard to remember.

This goes beyond the mere memorization of objects alone, as you will learn when you apply the key-words to remembering anecdotes, passages in books, and important subjects.

Historical dates become manageable with the application of this Figure Alphabet System. Key-lists are also provided with up to 100 code-words for further extension of this device.

The chapter is completed with explanations and illustrations of alternate methods in the form of a Picture Number System and a Phonetic Picture System, both readily learned.

The *Figure Alphabet* fits its name, but that requires a bit of explanation. It consists of figures, from 1 to 9 and 0, expressed in terms of certain letters. Since the purpose is to interpret each figure as fully as possible through letters, the alphabet taken is of the phonetic type, allowing choice of letters with a similar sound.

Moreover, those are all consonant sounds. Vowels were used in the early figure alphabets, but proved impractical or caused complications. For the modern form, they are utilized in an auxiliary fashion, so that the consonants form words.

As a simple example: In the Figure Alphabet, N is 2; M is 3. Thus, N-M would be 23. But since vowels are given no value, the word NAME (NaMe) is the equivalent of N-M and therefore would be 23. Also, NEW MAN (NeW MaN) would be 232, while MEAN MOON (MeaN MOON) would be 3232.

The standard Figure Alphabet runs as follows:
1 is T, TH or D, *because* T has one downstroke.
2 is N, *because* of its two downstrokes.
3 is M, with three downstrokes in written form.
4 is R, *as* FOUR has four letters, ending in R.
5 is L, the Roman numeral 50, which begins with 5.
6 is G, soft like J, CH, SH, *as* 6 looks like G.
7 is K, or hard C or G, *as* it resembles a key for K.
8 is F or V *as* the written F resembles a figure 8.
9 is P or B *as* the figure 9 resembles a reversed P.
0 is S or soft C *for* "cipher" and Z *for* "zero."
No figure values are assigned to the vowels, A,E,I,O,U, nor to W,H,Y.

No figure values are assigned to the vowels, A, E, I, O, U, nor to W, H, Y.

Once you have remembered these, you can express figures in words rather than letters. Thus TOE would be 1 (TOe) and so would ATE (aTe). NOW would be 2 (NOW) and so would ANY (aNy). Other words would apply with other figures. A more convenient procedure is to use a key list of words from "1 to 0", all having a common consonant, which helps keep them in mind.

Forming the Figure Alphabet
into a Working List

One of the best lists runs as follows:

1. HAT—haT—T	6. SHOE—SHOe—SH
2. HEN—heN—N	7. HOOK—hooK—K
3. HAM—haM—M	8. HOOF—hooF—F
4. HAIR—haiR—R	9. HOOP—hooP—P
5. HILL—hiLL—L	0. HOSE—hose—S

Note that a double letter counts as a single, phonetically, the "LL" in HILL representing "L." Also, as mentioned earlier, SH is the equivalent of soft G, so can be used instead, as in SHOE, which represents the figure 6 (G).

If you want to carry the list through 10 (instead of 0) the word DICE can represent that number. Its key consonants D-C (DICE) represent 1—D being the equivalent of T—and 0—as soft C is the equivalent of S.

The key-list can be fixed more solidly in mind by linking its units to form a mental chain. Thus you could picture a large HAT standing brim up, from which a HEN flies out, cackling happily. But instead of an egg being left behind, there is a HAM, which takes on the profile of a "ham" actor with long HAIR. This expands in such flowing style that it forms a HILL. On top of that is a big SHOE, to which a HOOK is attached and drawn away by a line tied to the HOOF of an animal like a donkey, which jumps through a flaming HOOP, and the fire is promptly extinguished by a HOSE.

For 10 (instead of 0) you could picture the hoop rolling about on a big table among a lot of tumbling giant DICE.

Advantages of H Series
as a Ten Word Code

As an added aid toward fixing this list in mind, the letter "H" has been used to start each key-word. The only exception is the word SHOE for 6. However, it includes the letter H in its phonetic key of SH, which in this case is the equivalent of the soft G, or J. Hence it is accepted in the "H" Series as this ten-word list may be termed.

Another advantage of using a special grouping like the "H Series" is this: Later, you can form other series of key-words from 1 to 10, utilizing identifying tabs for each. Examples of these will be given in due course. For the present, let us consider the "H Series" and its simple but amazingly potent use.

With this series of picture-words on immediate call, you have ten mental "pegs" for any odd group of objects that you may want to remember. If you are going to the hardware store to buy *paint, nails,* a *saw,* and a *stepladder,* you can think of a *hat* filled with *paint,* a *hen* pecking at *nails,* a *saw* being used to cut a *ham,* and a man whose beard—representing *hair*—is so long that he has to climb a *stepladder* to avoid tripping over it.

Such mental keys can be used over and over, for list after list. By extending key-words beyond the basic ten, you can memorize 20, 50, or even 100 "pegs"—according to how many you may require. This factor, too, will be covered later; but right now, let us see how effectively the simple ten word code—the "H Series"— can be applied in reading to remember.

Sample of Reading Material
Adaptable to Figure Alphabet

A good example is the following anecdote from the *Life Story* of P. T. Barnum. Skim through it, or read it rapidly; then jump to the analysis that follows it, showing how its ideas can be pegged in sequence by using the Figure Alphabet:

> It was my monomania to make my Museum the town wonder and town talk. As an illustration, one morning, a stout, hearty-looking man came into my ticket-office and begged some money. I asked him why he did not work and earn his living. He replied that he could get nothing to do and that he would be glad of any job at a dollar a day. I handed him a quarter of a dollar, told him to go and get breakfast and return, and I would employ him at light labor at a dollar and a half a day. When he returned I gave him five common bricks.

"Now," said I, "go and lay a brick on the sidewalk at the corner of Broadway and Ann Street; another close by the Museum; a third diagonally across the way at the corner of Broadway and Vesey Street, by the Astor House; put down the fourth on the sidewalk in front of St. Paul's Church, opposite; then, with the fifth brick in hand, take up a rapid march from one point to the other, making the circuit, exchanging your brick at every point, and say nothing to anyone."

"What is the object of this?" inquired the man.

"No matter," I replied; "all you need to know is that it brings you fifteen cents wage per hour. It is a bit of my fun, and to assist me properly you must seem to be deaf as a post; wear a serious countenance; answer no questions; pay no attention to anyone; but attend faithfully to the work and at the end of every hour by St. Paul's clock show this ticket at the Museum door; enter, walking solemnly through every hall in the building; pass out, and resume your work."

With the remark that it was "all one to him, so long as he could earn his living," the man placed his bricks and began his round. Half an hour afterwards, at least five hundred people were watching his mysterious movements. He had assumed a military step and bearing, and looking sober as a judge, he made no response whatever to the constant inquiries as to the object of his singular conduct.

At the end of the first hour, the sidewalks in the vicinity were packed with people all anxious to solve the mystery. The man, as directed, then went into the Museum, devoting fifteen minutes to a solemn survey of the halls, and afterwards returning to his round. This was repeated every hour till sundown and whenever the man went into the Museum a dozen or more persons would buy tickets and follow him, hoping to gratify their curiosity in regard to the purpose of his movements.

This was continued for several days—the curious people who followed the man into the Museum considerably more than paying his wages—till finally the policeman, to whom I had imparted my object, complained that the obstruction of the sidewalk by crowds had become so serious that I must call in my "brick man." This trivial incident excited considerable talk and amusement; it advertised me; and it materially advanced my purpose of making it a lively corner near the museum.

Analysis of Material
When Figure Alphabet is Used

Now to analyze the anecdote in terms of the Figure Alphabet, or Phonetic Numeral Code as it is also called. As already stated, the H series will be used. For this purpose, the story breaks down conveniently as follows:

Picture a HAT held in the hand of a beggar, who is asking Barnum for money. HAT and BEGGAR.

Picture a HEN that has laid an egg, with Barnum telling the man to lay down five bricks. HEN and BRICKS.

Picture the man as a HAM actor reaching the climax of his brick act at the end of each hour. HAM and HOUR.

Picture puzzled people running their fingers through their HAIR as they crowd about the man. HAIR and CROWD.

Picture the man going over a HILL leading gullible people like a pied piper, into the Museum. HILL and MUSEUM.

Picture a heavy SHOE moving along beside the man each time he stoops to resume his brick laying act. One shoe becomes another, representing a patrolling officer. SHOE and OFFICER.

Picture a HOOK catching the man's arm. The hook becomes the heavy hand of the law taking the man to Barnum. HOOK and LAW.

Picture a pounding HOOF that grows into an entire donkey, braying a loud, long laugh. The donkey can become successively a figure of Barnum, the beggar, the officer, and finally a crowd of donkeys all enjoying the joke. HOOF and JOKE.

Now read the article again, linking it with the pictures. Afterward, think of your key-words HAT, HEN and so on, pausing to let each picture form fully in mind. From them, each portion of the anecdote will not only be recalled; the details will be sharply etched, and you may remember some that you would otherwise miss.

After an interval of a day, a week, or even longer, any material thus "pegged" will often remain fresh and orderly, instead of being partly forgotten or confused. Frequently, you will hear some one start to tell a story, only to forget an important detail, get it mixed with something else, or get to the point too soon, thus spoiling the whole effect. That seldom happens if the story is fixed in mind through the Figure Alphabet device.

In the example just given—the Barnum anecdote—our purpose was simply to illustrate the use of these "picture pegs" as a memory aid. The anecdote itself is brief and simple enough to remember without using the Figure Alphabet device, although it is a help. Usually, the device is employed only when a story is somewhat lengthy and involved and must be remembered, or the material is of an otherwise important nature.

Utilizing the Figure
Alphabet on a Larger Scale

In Thoreau's *Walden,* there is a chapter on "The Village," describing life in the town near which he lived more than a century ago. In it, he starts by telling how he walked down to the village and what he saw on the way there. Then he talks about the people who spend all their time in idle chatter and gossip. Next, beginning with the grocery store, he enumerates the barroom, post office and bank as places of business; then he details others. He tells how the traveler is lured to spend his money, even being caught by the hair at the barber's.

Now, in reading the above, you can picture Thoreau putting on his HAT and observing things on the way to the village. There, the cackle of a HEN covers his discussion of local gossip. You see a HAM in the window of the grocery store, as a jog to the mercantile data that follows. Then, the key-word HAIR brings in the simile of the barber shop and all that it suggests.

Next follows a page or two that can be covered by the word HILL as it discusses life in the wilds and woods away from the village, almost like an interlude. Then, the windup, where Thoreau returned to the village to get a shoe from the cobbler's, is perfectly represented by the key-word SHOE. There, he was arrested for refusal to pay a tax—fitting with the word HOOK—and finally, he was released and returned to the woods, again free and footloose, well represented by the key-word HOOF.

Even without referring to the chapter mentioned, which runs some 2,000 words in length, it can be readily appreciated that the Figure Alphabet here provides nothing more than a skeleton key-list. Yet, that is sufficient for its purpose. It becomes a form of mental note-taking, breaking the chapter into subheads, which naturally may vary in length.

You can often apply this process in the course of serious reading, forming new picture pegs, like drawing a fresh breath, with each change of the subject. The material itself will have to be read carefully in its own right; but when you go back to review it, you will find that your skeleton key-list usually opens the proper locks as you come to them.

Applying the Figure Alphabet
to Enumerated Lists or Subjects

The Figure Alphabet reaches a high point of potential usefulness when you meet up with enumerated lists in the course of regular reading. In his *Autobiography*, Benjamin Franklin tells how he proposed moral virtues for himself, each with a short precept to express its extent of meaning.

Here are the first ten; and after reading them, you will find a way of remembering them through the Figure Alphabet:

1. TEMPERANCE—Eat not to dullness; drink not to elevation.
2. SILENCE—Speak not but what may benefit others or yourself; avoid trifling conversation.
3. ORDER—Let all your things have their places; let each part of your business have its time.
4. RESOLUTION—Resolve to perform what you ought; perform without fail what you resolve.
5. FRUGALITY—Make no expense but to do good to others or yourself; i.e., waste nothing.
6. INDUSTRY—Lose no time; be always employed in something useful; cut off all unnecessary actions.
7. SINCERITY—Use no hurtful deceit; think innocently and justly, and, if you speak, speak accordingly.
8. JUSTICE—Wrong none by doing injuries, or omitting the benefits that are your duty.

9. MODERATION—Avoid extremes; forbear resenting injuries so much as you think they deserve.
10. CLEANLINESS—Tolerate no uncleanliness in body, clothes, or habitation.

Now to use the pegs of the Figure Alphabet again. You can think of these as follows:

1. Think of Franklin putting on a HAT and leaving a tavern or a restaurant, as though he does not care to drink or eat. This ties in with TEMPERANCE.
2. Think of a cackling HEN which becomes quiet or subdued as it is stroked. This ties in with SILENCE.
3. Think of Franklin in a restaurant, saying he will have "an *order* of HAM." This ties in with ORDER.
4. Think of Franklin looking at himself in a mirror and combing his long HAIR with firmness and a look of resolution. This ties in with RESOLUTION.
5. Think of a big HILL. Picture Franklin in an automobile coasting down the hill past a gasoline station. At the bottom, he stops to count the pennies that he has saved by not using gas. This ties in with FRUGALITY.
6. Think of a SHOE, which—Franklin—or anyone else—is pegging, like a shoemaker in his window. This ties in with INDUSTRY.
7. Think of Franklin using his hand as a HOOK to draw a person close to him, but in a gentle way, so as to use no "hurtful" deceit. He is confiding in the person in a kindly way. This ties in with SINCERITY.
8. Think of a HOOF that keeps pounding until it changes into a judge's gavel, swung by Franklin. This ties in with JUSTICE.
9. Think of Franklin turning a large HOOP, showing that it has no ends, or "extremes." This ties in with MODERATION.

10. Think of DICE as something to be avoided, since people who play dice are frequently "cleaned" of their money. This ties in with CLEANLINESS.

Carrying the Code From
11 Through 20—and Beyond

The Figure Alphabet is not restricted to ten numbers. Your list can continue on from there; typical "pegs" from 11 to 20 are as follows:

11. DEED—DeeD—D-D	16. DISH—DiSH—D-SH
12. DOWN—DOWN—D-N	17. DECK—DecK—D-K
13. DAM—DaM—D-M	18. DOVE—DOVe—D-V
14. DEER—DeeR—D-R	19. DOPE—DOPe—D-P
15. DOLL—DOLL—D-L	20. NEWS—NewS—N-S

Observe that in this sequence, D is used instead of T to represent the figure 1. This is arbitrary; instead of DEED (DeeD) for 11, you could have DOT (DOT) or TOT (TOT) or even TODDY (T-D). The same applies to DOWN (DOWN) for 12 which could be TOWN (TOWN) or DUNE (DuNe) or TUNA (TuNa). Personal choices are also applicable to higher numbers.

However, a certain consistency in formation helps toward linkage. Thus in our "1 to 0" list, we used a silent "H" as an identifying tab. In 10 to 19, D is used for 1 instead of T, as stated. This can apply in higher brackets if the list is run up to 100, as J for figure 6 in the 60s, F for figure 8 in the 80s, P for figure 9 in the 90s.

At the same time, key words should be the sort that are easily pictured, or will fit nicely into an imaginary action. This has been given due consideration in the accompanying list, which provides keys from 1 to 100 inclusive. A good way to use such a list is to conform to it until you strike a word that seems awkward or does not suit your picturization. In that case, substitue an equivalent word of your own choice.

1	HAT		6	SHOE
2	HEN		7	HOOK
3	HAM		8	HOOF
4	HAIR		9	HOOP
5	HILL		10	DICE

11	DEED	41	ROAD	71	GATE
12	DOWN	42	RAIN	72	GUN
13	DAM	43	RAM	73	GUM
14	DEER	44	ROAR	74	GEAR
15	DOLL	45	RAIL	75	GALE
16	DISH	46	RICH	76	GASH
17	DECK	47	ROCK	77	GIG
18	DOVE	48	ROOF	78	GOOF
19	DOPE	49	ROPE	79	GOB
20	NEWS	50	LACE	80	FEZ
21	KNOT	51	LADY	81	FOOT
22	NUN	52	LAWN	82	FAN
23	NAME	53	LOOM	83	FOAM
24	NERO	54	LYRE	84	FIRE
25	NAIL	55	LILLY	85	FILE
26	NICHE	56	LASH	86	FISH
27	NECK	57	LOCK	87	FIG
28	KNIFE	58	LEAF	88	FIFE
29	KNOB	59	LIP	89	FOB
30	MOUSE	60	JUICE	90	PIZZA
31	MAT	61	JET	91	POT
32	MOON	62	GIN	92	PEN
33	MOM	63	JAM	93	POEM
34	MARE	64	JAR	94	PEAR
35	MAIL	65	JAIL	95	PAIL
36	MATCH	66	JUDGE	96	PATCH
37	MUG	67	JACK	97	PICK
38	MUFF	68	JOVE	98	PUFF
39	MAP	69	JAP	99	PIPE
40	RICE	70	GOOSE	100	DOSES

Extension and Uses
of the Code in Reading

While codes of 1 to 50, or those from 1 to 100 are useful with long lists of objects, or for special memory stunts, a shorter code will usually do when reading to remember. It is advisable to go beyond the simple limit of 1 to 10—say on through 11 to 20—because in regular reading, you may run into listings of a dozen or more maxims or rules.

Similarly, you may want to assure remembering chapter headings, which may run 20 or a few more. These are important in a survey or preview of a book, which may require keeping the overall contents more exactly in mind. It is quite feasible to "peg" a list of say 16 chapters, each with its identifying mental picture; then, in picking up a book, you can go quickly to the needed chapter without referring to the contents page at all.

Such practices depend upon individual readers as well as special purposes. They simply stress the availability of the Figure Alphabet, lending itself for a variety of purposes to the reader. Hence, as needed, the code may be enlarged.

Remembering Dates
Through the Figure Alphabet

One of the most widespread uses of the Figure Alphabet is in the remembering of dates. Here, you generally do best by forming a special mental picture—sometimes spontaneous, but often the result of careful consideration—that you tie in with the subject. As an appropriate example:

Columbus discovered America in 1492. He thought that he was bound for India. You can imagine a rather humorous, yet appropriate picture of Columbus putting on a Hindu turban as soon as he sighted land, in order to conform with the custom of the land. Link those two ideas: *Columbus—Turban.*

Now the word TURBAN, translated into the phonetic values of

the Figure Alphabet, as TURBaN, becomes T-1, R-4, B-9, N-2, giving the date of 1492.

Another opportune example is afforded by the life of George Washington, who was born 1732 and died in 1799. In such dates there is no need for the first two figures, as you already know the century. Practically then, Washington's birth and death may be regarded as '32 and '99.

Washington became a great man of his time. This suggests the word MAN as the first key, for his birth date. MaN is M-3, N-2, giving 32. When he died, he was the "Father of his Country." The term "father" reduces to PAPA. This "keys" as PaPa, with P-9 repeated, making 99.

Dates pertaining to Columbus and Washington are commonly known, because they have been drilled into the minds of many persons. Yet many of those same people bog down completely when asked to name the dates of birth and death of other important personages. The reason is, they dodge them, particularly in ordinary reading, thinking that they are hard to remember. This need not always be so, for you can now peg them home with the Figure Alphabet.

Take those of Benjamin Franklin, Edgar Allen Poe, Queen Victoria, Calvin Coolidge and Babe Ruth. Can you call off their dates? Or would you remember them, if you tried to commit them to memory by sheer rote, in the course of reading along? Probably not, but if you should pause and peg them in the following fashion, you would really have something novel to remember them by.

- BENJAMIN FRANKLIN was born in 1706 and died in 1790. He was a SAGE who lived to see his country at PEACE. SaGe becomes S-G or 06. PeaCe is 9-0 or 90.

- EDGAR ALLEN POE was born in 1809 and died at a comparatively young age in 1849. His great poem, *The Raven*, was published in 1845. Think of E. A. POE whose epitaph was simply R.I.P. E. A. Poe is simply P for 9 (09) and R.I.P. is

4-9 or 49. Picture the Raven sitting on a RAIL. RaiL—R-L— 45.

- QUEEN VICTORIA was born in 1819. She ascended the throne in 1837. She lived until 1901, having one of the longest reigns in history.

  Victoria was practically a debutante or DEB when she became a MEEK queen, who ascended the world's highest SEAT, the British throne. DEB is D-B or 19. MeeK is M-K or 37. seaT is S-T or 01.

- CALVIN COOLIDGE was born in 1872 and died in 1933. The "Cal" in his name represented his calculating nature; the "Cool" his calm, silent manner.

  Appropriately, Coolidge was a CANNY man who kept MUM. caNNy is hard C-N or 72. MuM is M-M or 33.

  Note: The term KEEN (KeeN) would do instead of CANNY.

- BABE RUTH, the "Home Run" king of modern baseball, was born in 1895 and died in 1948. He was famous for the tremendous distance that he could drive a baseball.

  Babe Ruth often hit the BALL over the ROOF.

  BaLL is B-L or 9-5 for 1895. ROOF is R-F or 48 for 1948.

Dates need not be difficult to remember when there is not enough time for normal associations. On those occasions, you could fix a firm phonetic picture with them. In addition, the more the picture grows, the harder it is to forget the dates.

Several Points in Use of Figure Alphabet—with Illustrations

Two important points should be noted with the use of the Figure Alphabet for dates and statistical purposes:

- *First*, Figure pictures thus formed do not interfere with the regular use of the Figure Alphabet word code. For instance, suppose that you should memorize the Presidents of the United States by means of the 1 to 50 code. Your key-word HAT would represent Washington wearing a hat; HEN would be John Adams cackling like a hen; HAM is short for Hamilton whose influence made Jefferson president.

That brings you to HAIR, representing the fourth president, James Madison, who is tugging at his hair in a "mad" fashion because of war problems with England. Carrying this further, there is something else that makes little "Maddy" more than a little mad. He wants a LIGHT but he can't find a MATCH. LiGhT (pronounced LiTe) is L-T or 51 for 1751, the year of Madison's birth. MaTCH (pronounced MaCH) is M-CH or 3-6 for 1836, the year of his death.

Systems Used in Combination

• *Second,* the Figure Alphabet can be used for dates as an adjunct to some other device, such as the Room System or the Chain System. For a good example, check back to the account of the origin and development of the "Room System" in the previous chapter, with the list showing its application. (See page 139.)

There we used eight "locations" and with three of these, dates were given, involving specific persons; but in applying the "Room System" in those cases, only the names were fixed, as follows:

Location 1.   Simonides. (Bust on phone table.)
Location 5.   Roger Bacon. (Bacon on writing desk.)
Location 7.   Winkelmann. (Winking over bookcase.)

Now, the dates in those cases were Simonides, 470 B.C.; Bacon, 1214, A.D.; Winkelman, 1648. To remember these handily, you have only to add to the picture, in terms of the Figure Alphabet, utilizing a descriptive word that incorporates the date. For example:

• LOCATION 1:   *The telephone table.*
Visualize a pile of rocks (ROCKS) on the table, with the bust of Simonides perched upon that. The rocks are the added item

and the words ROCKS consists of R-4, K-7, S-0, giving the date of 470, which flashes on as 470 B.C.

• LOCATION 5:   *The writing desk.*

We have already visualized a plate of appetizing bacon. Make it *tender bacon,* incorporation TENDER as the added item. Its letters, T-1, N-2, D-1, R-4, give the date of 1214, the year in which Roger Bacon was born.

• LOCATION 7:   *The bookcase.*

We already have Winkelmann wisely winking at us, and the question may naturally arise: What was Winkelmann? The answer is: *A teacher of* mnemonics.

By taking the first words of that phrase—A TEACHER OF—and reducing it to phonetics, you have: a TeaCHeR oF. That results in T-1, CH-6, R-4, F-8, producing the year 1648, when Winkelmann introduced his system.

Note: The date pertaining to Ravennas, at Location 6, *The picture window,* was already pegged more naturally by associating him with Columbus, as of 1491, the year before Columbus set sail.

It could be fixed with the Figure Alphabet instead, by thinking of Ravennas receiving a letter that begins: "Dear Pete." The words DEAR PETE key as DeaR PeTe, with D-1, R-4, P-9, T-1, giving the required 1491.

How to "Peg"
Varied Types of Data

Names, addresses, telephone numbers, and many other useful items, can all be fixed or recalled through the Figure Alphabet. The more you use this system, the more skillfull you will become with it and the more you will appreciate its possibilities.

Just as reading techniques can be improved by the methods given earlier in this volume, so can memory skills be augmented by the systems outlined in the last two chapters. The faster you are able to read, the more you will find yourself remembering, and the better you will be synchronizing the two processes.

Often, in reading, you will pause and try to fix an important passage in mind. If the pause is becoming too long, you can apply an artificial memory device, and very likely remember the material more effectively. The time otherwise spent in using sheer rote with little result, may bring big results if the Figure Alphabet is judiciously employed.

Sometimes with dates and various complex data, you may want to read on and come back later to pick up the more involved material. In such cases, you will also find that use of a system may be a valuable time saver.

There is a special advantage in learning some of the higher brackets of the 1 to 100 Word Code, where reading to remember is concerned. In our ten-word code, we have concentrated on the "H Series" which gives the key-words 1 to 10 a conformity that aids in their memorization.

Now, if this "H Series" is used constantly whenever you memorize up to ten objects, you will have everything beginning with HAT and running through HEN, HAM and so on. Actually, that is no great disadvantage if you "key" your first picture. Ben Franklin wearing his hat starts one chain; Thoreau wearing a hat starts another.

However, if you have other series available, you can switch from H Series (1 to 10) to another like the M Series (31 to 40) or the R Series (41 to 50) or even higher.

There are other forms of the 1 to 10 "picture system" that are useful in reading to remember, where short lists are concerned. Two of these are given here, because of the ease with which they can be learned and their adaptability to mental picturization.

Simple Picture-Number System as Substitute for Figure Alphabet

Here, you visualize the numbers 1 to 10 as actual objects, running in order and shaped as described.

1 is a *Candle,* tall, thin, like the figure 1.

2 is a *Swan,* swimming in the water, bending its neck gracefully, like the figure 2.

3 is a *Pitchfork* or Trident, with its prongs pointing to the left, like the figure 3.

4 is a *Pennant* or pointed Flag, flying from its staff to represent the figure 4.

5 is a *Hand,* with thumb and fingers spread, showing five digits—with only thumb and fingers extended, it represents the Roman numeral V for "five."

6 is a *Snake,* coiled with raised head, like a 6.

7 is a *Semaphore* or Railway Signal, which with its post looks like a 7.

8 is an *Hourglass* which conforms nicely to 8.

9 is a *Mailbox* on its post, resembling the figure 9.

10 is composed of a KNIFE and PLATE like the figures 1 and 0. Remove the knife, you have the PLATE for 0.

As a sample application of these pictures, suppose that you used the first four to remember the "Four Freedoms" as enumerated by President Franklin D. Roosevelt. Your quick-pics could run as follows:

1. Picture a *candle* in a lantern held by a patriot in Colonial costume as he reads a proclamation or makes an announcement.
   Freedom of Speech

2. Visualize a *swan,* gracefully bowing and dipping its head as if in prayer.
   Freedom of Worship

3. Picture a man with a *pitchfork,* busily loading a wagon with hay, from a big haystack, with corn, cattle, other signs of plenty all around.
   Freedom from Want

4. Picture a pennant flying at the head of a bold group of charging men, or above a great fort.
Freedom from Fear

Another Substitute— the Phonetic Picture System

Another list of ten handy words is based on the *sounds* of the numbers from 1 to 10. That makes them easy to remember, but to have them ready for use, a series of established pictures should accompany them.

The list runs:

1. WON which sounds like ONE.
   A runner crossing a finish line.
2. TUBE which sounds like TWO (B).
   A metal tube open at both ends.
3. TREE which sounds like THREE.
   A scrawny tree with just three branches.
4. FORT which sounds like FOUR(T).
   A fort with four walls.
5. FIFE which sounds like FIVE.
   A fife being played by thumb and fingers.
6. STICKS which sounds like SIX.
   Think of six sticks, going with the rhyme: "Four, five, *six—* pick up *sticks.*"
7. HEAVEN which sounds like SEVEN.
   Think of a "seventh heaven" with a cluster of stars in the sky.
8. WEIGHT which sounds like (W)EIGHT.
   A heavy weight, balancing a scale.
9. DINE which sounds like NINE.
   A restaurant table with a clock saying nine.
10. TENT which sounds like TEN(T).
    Imagine a tent. Take away its pole (the figure 1) and it collapses into nothing (0).

As an illustration of how this list can be used, suppose that you are reading an article by a naturalist who has studied the intelligence of various animals with respect to a special problem. In this situation, he regards the elephant as the most intelligent of the group he observed, with the horse coming second, the dog a close third, and after that, the beaver, cat and seal in the order given, making six in all.

You could then picture:

> 1. An elephant race, with one leading the herd across the finish line. 2. A parade of horses going through a tunnel shaped like a big tube. 3. A dog barking up at the lower branches of a tree. 4. A group of beavers building a log fort. 5. A cat playing a fife. 6. A trained seal picking up sticks.

Using word games to strengthen reading retention

X

The use of special word games in reading to remember is a special subject in itself. Starting with old-time word puzzles, it leads into the more modern "crosswords" which always retain their popularity.

How crosswords can be used to advantage, is shown by a comparison of crossword types, covering those that partially fulfill fivefold qualifications pertaining to word and sentence structure.

These qualifications are further stressed through recommended games which just about meet the major needs. A series of such games and their variants make up the main portion of this chapter.

How the games can be played singly, with teams, or with groups, is amply explained, along with suggestions for continued or more advanced play. All these games have been specially selected as aids toward reading to remember.

Games and puzzles involving words have long been valuable in building vocabulary and sharpening memory. In our earlier chapters, we have suggested and covered some of these. The formation and recognition of acronyms and acrostics come directly into this category; while other phases of reading and remembering, including artificial memory aids, provide an incentive similar to games.

How much can word games help you to read faster and remember more? They may help a great deal, provided they are judiciously used. Otherwise, the time devoted to such pastimes might be better spent reading. They should be balanced, so to speak, rather than leaning to one type. Also to be taken into account is that some games have advantages over others as will be seen.

There are certain aims to be achieved through word games and puzzles, so by mixing the games, you can cover the variety of phases. They have been grouped under five representative heads:

1. Word recognition
2. Word building
3. Sentence structure
4. Filling in sentences
5. Identifying subject matter

The old-syle wordsquares, acrostics and other formations, were very limited in scope and usually represented long struggles with little used words. They helped in word recognition and word building, but it took a scholar or a dedicated enthusiast to work through them, rather than an average reader. The advent of the modern crossword puzzle changed that, giving greater flexibility and expanse to word recognition and word building, but doing little to help the other points, unless a singular effort is made.

Using Crosswords to Good
Advantage in Reading to Remember

Certain words have come to be termed "crossword puzzle words" because you seldom see them elsewhere. The *ai,* meaning the three-toed sloth, is a good example. But how many puzzlers have ever encountered a three-toed sloth? Or still more to the point, how many thousands of persons who are familiar with ai, can tell you the name of its close cousin, the two-toed sloth?

It happens to be the unau, and you may have to find it in a larger dictionary, but the unau is badly neglected because it is so seldom needed in a puzzle. Many similar cases could be cited, showing how the crossword puzzle is somewhat warped or deficient where vocabulary improvement is concerned. Indeed, there are many critics who feel that the native names of any sloths, whether two or three-toed, are hardly essential to a good vocabulary.

Actually, the bane of many puzzlers, abbreviations, constitute a most valuable phase of crosswords. It may be said that the less abbreviations, the better a puzzle is, that is, as a puzzle. From another standpoint, the more abbreviations that a puzzle contains, the more you learn from it. This is very useful in our modern day of acronyms, coined words and the like.

Some puzzlers shun crosswords with "tricky" definitions, but those are the sort that aid in sentence structure, fill-ins and ability to identify subject matter. For example, name a four-letter word meaning *worst*. The answer happens to be *best*. When "worst" and "best" are used as verbs, they have an identical meaning; as:

Sir Lancelot *worsted* all the knights he encountered.

Sir Lancelot *bested* all the knights he encountered.

Some crossword puzzles utilize sentences in definitions, sometimes with gaps to be filled in by the proper word. These go into sentence structure, fill-ins and subject matter; hence, they are particularly worthy. In short, don't stay in the crossword rut, doing the same restricted types of puzzles over and over, with all the old familiars of ai, ere, kiwi, Erin, Iran, Enid, Eros, Aries, Iris, Isis, and all that hackneyed list. Go after puzzles that offer new challenges and techniques.

Adapting Other Word Games
to Reading and Remembering

At the same time, avoid being bogged down. Cryptograms, with their letter substitutions, are a good pastime, as solving them demands both word and sentence recognition. However, inveterate cryptogram solvers can easily spend hours over nonsensical, almost impossible phrases which are meant to trap them and may actually impair their reading ability rather than improve it.

Strictly speaking, all forms of word games and puzzles are good to a degree, but care should be taken in choosing them. You can drop those that become outworn, and switch to games of varied types in order to gain the benefit of those which are helpful to the different headings, as given earlier in this chapter.

The word games and puzzles that follow have been particularly selected with this purpose in mind and to tie in with factors of reading to remember.

GAMES, PUZZLES

1. HIDDEN WORD HUNT
   (a) Hidden Cities
   (b) Hidden States
   (c) Hidden Birds
   (d) Hidden Trees
2. CATEGORIES
3. WORD CHANGE GAME
4. WORD LINK GAME

5. THE KEY-WORD GAME
   (a) End Each Word
   (b) Middle of the Worders
   (c) Begin Each Word
   (d) Zigzag Words
6. THE GAME OF GHOSTS
7. THE PALINDROME GAME
8. THE ANAGRAM GAME

(*Answers follow each section as needed.*)

HIDDEN WORD HUNT

Here is a game that fits the process of word recognition, acting as an aid in reading to remember. The shape of a word, its oddities, any components such as shorter words, all are helpful when noted, as they alert the reader.

Years ago, a game came into vogue, that of framing "trick" sentences to conceal the name of a person, thing or place, although its letters were kept in their proper order. As an example, the name of a wild animal is contained in the following sentence:

Being shy enables you to study nature.

The answer, indicated by italics, is HYENA:

Being s*hy ena*bles you to study nature.

Now, we have gone the old game not "just one better," but a dozen or more better, by including a whole series of related words in single paragraphs. The general statements themselves are a bit vague or slightly nonsensical, but that only adds to the interest, as odd word combinations are sometimes necessary to work in hidden names.

Hence, those may serve as clues, but there are other phrases that may seem just as promising yet which may mislead you. Now that you know the game, you can proceed from there.

HIDDEN CITIES

The names of 14 American cities are hidden in the following paragraph. Some are state capitals and the rest are well known, mostly with populations of 100,000 or more.

We collect rent on Monday to nullify people who say, "Hello, we'll pay later" but never do very much about it. If you grab Al, Tim or Ed when you see them, you meet with a rebuff a lot of times. They keep their thoughts hidden very closely, but when I am not excited but am patient, it would seem I am interested in them, so there are no far gone conclusions to be drawn and we have a lot of sport landing fish together. When I buy a sandwich I take it with me and the crowd all asked me to bring some for them. They must think I'm Santa Claus, tinsel and all!

HIDDEN STATES

There are 50 states in the Union and you will find the names of 13 hidden in the paragraph that follows. Not the original 13, but some are old and some are new, while some are large and some are small. Try to find them.

I took grandma in every exhibit at the Fair, but a halt came when we saw a marshal ask an officer about the India national display. We could no more go nicely on our way before grandma tried to dismiss our itinerary as useless. Still, I noisily insisted it was good.

That exasperated her and she asked, as though her words made law, "Are you going to argue over months instead of days?" So I stayed in the patio watching the fiesta and after all became placid, a homely thought struck me: "When you eat fried chicken tuck your napkin in your collar!"

HIDDEN BIRDS

The paragraph below discusses fishing and brings up some unusual angles that have very little to do with the subject. In fact, you shouldn't think of fish at all while you read it. Think of birds, as there are a dozen of them hidden there, as nicely as if they were perched deep in the branches of a tree. See how many you can spot!

When the sea gleams, fish awkwardly nose from the water nibbling bait. By being quick, I will catch them. A few renew their efforts with rushing tactics, but only stragglers nip eagerly. So when you roll to Rio leave your fishing gear at home. Let no stray fin challenge your skill on deck. To be popular keep below letting some other onlooker waste his time.

HIDDEN TREES

While you read through the following narrative, look for trees. Unless the woods prove so thick that you can't see them, you may find as many as 14. All fairly common or well-known trees, each with its letters in correct order.

A bee chased the bony horse and it pranced around while we studied polar charts shown on the map left by the rebel militia. We drank soda pop largely to pass the time and began to spin exaggerated yarns. Some held erratic notions, claiming fire buckets would be safer if we kept them locked up, while others found banging cymbals amusing, tho' akin to stupidity, for which we will owe our thanks.

ANSWERS

• HIDDEN CITIES: We collecT RENT ON monDAY TO Nullify people who say, "helLO WE'LL pay later but never DO VERy much about it. If you graB AL, TIM OR Ed when you see them, you meet with a reBUFF A LOt of times. They keep their thoughts hidDEN VERY closely, but when I am not excited buT AM PAtient, it would seeM I AM INterested in them so there aRE NO FAR GOne conclusions to be drawn and we have a lot of SPORT LANDing fish together. When I buy a sandWICH I TAke it with me and the crowD ALL ASked me to bring some for them. They must think I'm Santa ClAUS TINsel and all!

1. TRENTON. 2. LOWELL. 3. DOVER. 4. BALTIMORE. 5. BUF-FALO. 6. DENVER 7. TAMPA. 8. MIAMI. 9. RENO. 10. FARGO. 11. PORTLAND 12. WICHITA. 13. DALLAS. 14. AUSTIN.

• HIDDEN STATES: I took grandMA IN Every exhibit at the fair, buT A Halt came when we saw a marshAL ASK An officer about the INDIA NAtional display. We could no mORE GO Nicely on our way before grandma tried to disMISS OUR Itinerary as useless. StILL, I NOIsily insisted it was good. ThaT EXASperated her and she asked, as though her words maDE LAW, "ARE you going to argue OVER MONThs instead of days?" So I stayed in the patIO WAtching the fiesta and after all became placID A HOmely thought struck me: "When you eat fried chicKEN TUCK YOUr napkin in your collar!"

1. MAINE. 2. UTAH. 3. ALASKA. 4. INDIANA. 5. OREGON. 6. MISSOURI. 7. ILLINOIS. 8. TEXAS. 9. DELAWARE. 10. VERMONT. 11. IOWA. 12. IDAHO. 13. KENTUCKY.

• HIDDEN BIRDS: When the SEA GLEams, fisH AWKwardly nose from the waTER Nibbling at bait. By being quicK I WIll catch them. A few RENew their efforts wiTH RUSHing tactics, but only stragglers NIP Eagerly. So when you roll to RIO LEave your fishing gear home. Let no stray FIN CHallenge your skill on deck. To be popuLAR Keep below Letting some OtHER ONlooker waste his time.

1. EAGLE. 2. HAWK. 3. TERN. 4. KIWI. 5. WREN. 6. THRUSH. 7. SNIPE. 8. ORIOLE. 9. FINCH. 10. LARK. 11. OWL. 12. HERON.

• HIDDEN TREES: A BEE CHased thE BONY horse and it pranceED ARound while we studied poLAR CHarts shown on the MAP LEft by the rebEL MIlitia. We drank soda POP LARgely to pass the time and began to SPIN EXaggerated yarns. Some hELD ERratic notions, claiming FIRE buckets would be safer if we kept tHEM LOCKed up, while others found banging cymBALS AMusing, tho' AKin to stupidity, for which we WILL OWe our thanks.

1. BEECH. 2. EBONY. 3. CEDAR. 4. LARCH. 5. MAPLE. 6. ELM. 7. POPLAR. 8. PINE. 9. ELDER. 10. FIR. 11. HEMLOCK. 12. BALSAM. 13. OAK. 14. WILLOW.

CATEGORIES

Also known as Guggenheim, this is an excellent game for avid readers as it requires thinking of words, often in the form of pictures, and recalling them as well. Hence, as a supplementary activity in the art of reading to remember, it can be highly appropriate.

In perhaps its most practical form, the game is played as follows:

Each player is given a sheet of paper with five cross-rows divided in five vertical sections, as illustrated. Five groups of objects or items bearing some definite similarity within each group, are chosen as "categories" and these are listed, one to each cross-row. (See pages 182-183.)

For example: Authors, rivers, State Capitals, makes of automobiles, foreign words, generals, chemical elements, monsters, nations, lakes, birds, trees, musical instruments, even the street names of a particular city, are all suitable.

Next, a special word is chosen, containing five letters. It is a good idea to write a number of these words on cards and mix them; then choose one. Or someone may open a book to a random page and take the first five-letter word that comes along. Suppose that the categories chosen are Flowers, Lakes, State Capitols, Words containing the letter X, Islands, Chemical Elements.

Those would be written at the left of each cross row. Next, the special word would be chosen. Assume it to be the word RIGHT. Its letters R-I-G-H-T are set separately above each vertical column.

Each player would then have a chart like that appearing on page 182.

A time limit is set, say ten minutes, and with the signal to start, each player begins filling in his spaces with descriptive words beginning with the proper letters. Thus, at the end of the time limit, a sheet might look like the one on page 183.

This player has filled 24 out of 25 spaces, which in this case represents the greatest possible capacity, because there is no state capital beginning with the letter G. That adds special interest to the game. If a player is doubtful whether a certain category can be filled, he can go on to others and fill them instead. Meanwhile, his opponents may be wasting their time looking for a word that doesn't exist.

In scoring this game, it is not simply a question of who fills the most spaces. The idea is to find unusual words and thereby out-guess the opponents. This means that when a player is well along with his list, he can begin to change it, if there still is time. For example, "rose'" is perhaps the most obvious of all flowers be-ginning with the letter "R," so it would be advisable to erase it and put a flower like "rhododendron" in its place.

With state capitals, the letter "T" offers "Trenton" or "Talla-hassee" instead of "Topeka," so if a player thinks of all three, he should weigh them somewhat before making his final choice, always thinking in terms of the opposing players and what their choices may be.

This helps toward a winning score, as at the finish, the lists are compared and words are counted as follows:

For each correct word, a player scores 1 point for each list that does not have it. Thus, in a five person game, if only one player wrote down "rhododendron," he would score 4 points. If the others all wrote "rose," they would score 1 point each.

If, under State Capitals, all five players put down "Richmond" as their "R," there would be no score for anyone. If, however, two players failed to think of "Richmond," which is the only available

	R	I	G	H	T
Flowers					
Lakes					
State Capitals					
Words with Letter X					
Chemical Elements					

"R" and failed to fill that box, the other three players would score 2 points each.

With composite or doubtful words, it is best to give the player just 1 point. Under "Lakes," "Great Salt Lake" would rate a full score, because that is its actual name. But if a player put down "red clover" under "R" in the "Flower" category, it would be doubtful. Actually, "clover" is the flower, though "red clover" is a species. On this occasion, it should receive 1 point.

	R	**I**	**G**	**H**	**T**
Flowers	Rose	Iris	Gardenia	Hyacinth	Tulip
Lakes	Red Lake	Itaska	Great Salt Lake	Huron	Titicaca
State Capitals	Richmond	Indian-apolis	—	Helena	Topeka
Words with Letter X	reflex	ibex	galaxy	hexagon	tax
Chemical Elements	radium	iron	gold	helium	tungsten

To allow more than 1 point for such words might spoil the game, as some players might go after freakish combinations, knowing that other persons would not be using them.

In any case, "Categories" is real fun and a great vocabulary activator as well, because you may have to probe mentally through long lists of words before striking the one you need.

WORD CHANGE GAME

This is an excellent diversion, both as a solo puzzle or a group game. The main purpose is to "change" one word into another that is somewhat related to it—as COLD to WARM—by substituting one new letter at a time, and forming a new word with each step.

Thus, from COLD to WARM, your sequence could run as shown here, requiring six words in all. But while that fulfills the requirements, namely, a new word with each letter change, the result might be accomplished in less steps. Trying for that becomes part of the game, too.

COLD
CORD
CARD
HARD
HARM
WARM

With several players all working on the same "Word Change," a time limit can be set, and whoever comes up with the shortest list is the winner. He can either be credited with one game in a series, or given points according to the margin of his win. The series can then continue with new words until someone reaches 10 points. Here, we see COLD changed to WARM in five words, beating the previous effort by one word.

COLD
WOLD
WORD
WARD
WARM

WORD CHANGE #1

H A R D

Change HARD to ROCK

– – – –

– – – –

– – – –

– – – –

– – – –

– – – –

– – – –

– – – –

R O C K

For convenience, sheets should be made up with blank spaces—more than will normally be needed—in which players can insert the transition words. Ten spaces are given here—including the words HARD and ROCK—but you should be able to make the change in less.

Word Change #2

F I S H   Change FISH to MEAT

- - - -

- - - -   Again, spaces are provided, though you may

- - - -   not have to use them all. Often, the crucial point

- - - -   of this game lies in the first change, or the next to

- - - -   last. There, choices are sometimes quite limited, and

- - - -   one may produce a short course, another a long one.

- - - -

- - - -

- - - -

- - - -

M E A T

Word Change #3

The ancient alchemists spent centuries   I R O N - - - -

trying to change IRON into GOLD, so don't   - - - -   - - - -

expect to accomplish it too rapidly!   - - - -   - - - -

Names of countries, places and people   - - - -   - - - -

are allowable in these word changes—other-   - - - -   - - - -

wise you'd never get off the ground with   - - - -   - - - -

this one.   - - - - G O L D

Word Change #4

B L A C K - - - - -   For persons who try to talk you

- - - - -   - - - - -   into believing that "black is white,"

- - - - -   - - - - -   here is their chance to prove it, by

- - - - -   - - - - -   changing BLACK to WHITE in the fewest

- - - - -   - - - - -   possible steps. It may take more than

- - - - -   - - - - -   they expect, so this is apt to be well

- - - - - W H I T E   contested.

Word Change #5

Changing DOCK to SHIP should be rapid, if you get off to the right start. But some of these can be tricky, so allow enough spaces. This is the type where one lucky player may undercut another nicely and make a good score.

DOCK _ _ _ _
_ _ _ _   _ _ _ _
_ _ _ _   _ _ _ _
_ _ _ _   _ _ _ _
_ _ _ _   _ _ _ _
_ _ _ _   _ _ _ _
_ _ _ _   _ _ _ _
_ _ _ _   _ _ _ _
_ _ _ _   _ _ _ _
_ _ _ _   SHIP

Word Change #6

In all these "Word Change Games," plurals, past tenses and adjectival forms may be used as desired. Thus BONE could become BONY, or SWORE become SWORN. This, along with proper names, gives flexibility to the game.

You will need it in changing SPOON to GLASS, which requires some rather difficult shifts.

SPOON _ _ _ _ _
_ _ _ _ _   _ _ _ _ _
_ _ _ _ _   _ _ _ _ _
_ _ _ _ _   _ _ _ _ _
_ _ _ _ _   _ _ _ _ _
_ _ _ _ _   _ _ _ _ _
_ _ _ _ _   _ _ _ _ _
_ _ _ _ _   _ _ _ _ _
_ _ _ _ _   _ _ _ _ _
_ _ _ _ _   _ _ _ _ _
_ _ _ _ _   _ _ _ _ _
_ _ _ _ _   _ _ _ _ _
_ _ _ _ _   _ _ _ _ _
_ _ _ _ _   GLASS

ANSWERS

Word Change #1

HARD to ROCK

HARD	HARD
LARD	HARK
LARK	HACK
LACK	RACK
LOCK	ROCK
ROCK	*(Only 5*
(6 steps)	*steps)*

Word Change #2

FISH to MEAT

FISH	*That can*	*While one*
DISH	*be beaten*	*less is*
DASH	*by:*	*needed with:*
LASH	FISH	FISH
LAST	FIST	FIST
PAST	MIST	FIAT
PEST	MOST	FEAT
PEAT	MOAT	MEAT
MEAT	MEAT	

Word Change #3

IRON to GOLD

The first two steps are "musts" but after that, variations are possible.

IRON	IRON
IRAN	IRAN
BRAN	BRAN
BEAN	BRAD
BEAT	BEAD
BOAT	READ
BOLT	ROAD
BOLD	GOAD
GOLD	GOLD

Word Change #4

BLACK to WHITE

BLACK	BLACK
SLACK	BLANK
SLICK	BLINK
CLICK	CLINK
CRICK	CHINK
TRICK	THINK
TRICE	THINE
TRITE	WHINE
WRITE	WHITE
WHITE	*(One step less)*

Word Change #5

DOCK to SHIP

DOCK	*In contrast*
HOCK	*to 15 words*
HACK	*at the left,*
PACK	*here is a*
PACT	*quick play:*
PART	DOCK
PARD	SOCK
PAID	SOAK
SAID	SOAP
SLID	SLAP
SLED	SLIP
SHED	SHIP
SHOD	
SHOP	
SHIP	

Word Change #6

SPOON to GLASS

Real long ones!

SPOON	SPOON
SPOOL	SWOON
SPOIL	SWORN
SPILL	SHORN
SPELL	SHORE
SHELL	SHARE
SHALL	SHARK
SHALE	SHANK
STALE	THANK
STOLE	THINK
STONE	THICK
SHONE	TRICK
SHINE	TRACK
THINE	CRACK
TRINE	CRANK
TRIPE	CLANK
TRIPS	CLANS
DRIPS	CLASS
DROPS	GLASS
DROSS	
GROSS	
GRASS	
GLASS	

WORD LINK GAME

There are two participants in this intriguing game. One player, *A*, has a list of five words, all of a descriptive nature. It is his purpose to convey those words to player *B*, through use of synonyms or related words. If he manages this on the first try, 10 points are scored. If he fails, another try is allowed, with 9 points for a correct call. Otherwise, there are successive tries at 8, 7, 6 and so on down until *A*'s word is named by *B*.

The object is to score as high a total as possible with a given number of words. Using five words to a game, the best possible score would be 50. The lowest, consisting of five outright failures, would be 0.

The following examples fully illustrate the play.

The word chosen by *A* is BLISTER.

(10) *A* gives the related word SORE.   *B* responds with HEAD.
(9) *A* gives the related word PAIN.   *B* responds with HEADACHE.
(8) *A* gives the related word HURT.   *B* responds with WOUND.
(7) *A* gives the related word SKIN.   *B* responds with CUT.
(6) *A* gives the related word SMOOTH.   *B* responds with BRUISE.
(5) *A* gives the related word BULGE.   *B* responds with BLISTER.

That is finally correct, so 5 points are scored, as indicated in the parentheses.

As another example, *A* chooses WEDDING.

(10) *A* gives the related word BELL.   *B* responds with CHURCH.
(9) *A* gives the related word BRIDE.   *B* responds with GROOM.
(8) *A* gives the related word BOTH.   *B* responds with MARRIAGE.
(7) *A* gives the related word CEREMONY. *B* responds with WEDDING.

That is correct, so in this case 7 points are scored.

It will be noted that the quest narrows with successive words and that in some cases "leading" terms are used, rather than those which are synonymous or closely related.

In the first example, after "skin" brought "cut," *A*'s suggestion "smooth" was intended as a clue to the condition of the skin, and caused *B* to switch to "bruise." *A*'s use of "bulge" was a descriptive term, and instead, *A* could have used "burst," or gone on with the next. As it was, *B* came up with "blister."

In the second example, the leading word was "both," whereby *A* conveyed the idea that *both* the bride and groom were included in the main word, which was "wedding." If instead, *A* had used the word "ring," it might have given the idea of both bride and groom, provided that *B* had pictured a wedding ring. But if *B* had accepted "ring" as a verb, to denote a ringing sound, his thought train might have reverted to the word "bell" which was suggested earlier.

Numerous examples could be given to show the surprises and twists of this game, but those can best be appreciated by playing it yourself, and thus gaining the benefit of the many phases of word recognition that it offers. This is excellent exercise broadening reading scope. The main word should be specially chosen to allow for varied links, yet at the same time it should be an easy word to picture.

Here are suitable types:

> Buggy, Couch, Crate, Fortune, House, Hungry, Hunter, Indian, Kangaroo, Kitten, Leopard, Mitten, Orange, Pail (Pale) Purse, Ruler, Soda, Tug, Usher, Victory, Xylophone, Zebra, Zone.

One good way to insure a proper variety of words is to write out a large list on separate cards or slips of paper. These are mixed and Player *A* then picks out five at random, conveying them singly to Player *B,* as specified. The game can also be played on a "turnabout" basis, with *B* picking words and conveying them to *A*. Each series should be the same length—say, five—so as to aim for the same top score of 50.

In the form just described, the game is not competitive, as both players are working together. They can make it a case of "beating the clock," if they wish, by setting a limit, such as 30 seconds, for each response. Thus the word "Blister" would have been reached in less than three minutes; and "Ceremony" in less than two, if the "time limit" had been applied in the cases given. Player *A* would watch the clock, while giving cues to Player *B*.

Still better, a third player can act as timekeeper and referee. This person picks the words, shows them to *A*, who gives links to *B*

in the usual fashion. But if 30 seconds go by, the timekeeper tells
A to name another link, without waiting for *B*'s response to the
previous one. The third person also can rule out any leads that
may be giveaways, or multiple terms, such as "judge's hammer"
for "gavel."

As a competitive game, two teams are needed, one consisting
of Players *A* and *B*, the other of another pair, *C* and *D*. The time-
keeper-referee, Mr. *X*, then runs the game. He gives the *A* and *B*
team a chance at one word; then does the same with *C* and *D*,
who are given another word. The team scoring the highest total in
an equal number of games is the winner.

THE KEY-WORD GAME

In the "Key-word Game, the play itself is intriguing while
at the same time it serves as a test of word recognition. One person
can play it as a puzzle game, timing himself to see how long it
takes to fill in each list. Or, a group can play it as a contest, each
person being supplied with a duplicate list. The one getting the
most words right within a set time limit becomes the winner.

Four variants of the "Key-word" Game appear in the lists
that follow. In *Game A,* you have the "key-word" CAL as the
beginning of each word. Your job is to add more letters, filling the
extra spaces, so that you end each word according to the definition
given with it. This is the easiest form of the game, because your
"key" gives you a starting syllable.

In *Game B,* your "key-word" EAT is in the middle of each
word, for the first group of six. It becomes ART in the second
group. The procedure is the same, but you must visualize two
letters that start each word, along with two to finish it.

In *Game C,* you need starting letters for each word. The gap
consists of three letters in each of the first nine words; with the
final six, there is a five letter gap at the start. All the endings are
exactly the same, TRY in each case.

In *Game D,* each "key-word" operates in zigzag fashion,

occupying a different portion of the word in which it appears. This is perhaps the most fascinating form of the game and also the most deceptive, as that shift in position can make quite a difference in pronunciation and also the number of syllables.

Just as examples of the "key-word" usage, take these cases involving the "key-word" ERA:

(a) E R A _ _ _   Something that eradicates
(b) _ _ _ _ E R A   A fanciful monster
(c) _ _ _ E R A _ _ _   As a customary thing

The answers are (a) ERASER (b) CHIMERA (c) GENERALLY.

That gives a sufficient idea to proceed with the games that follow. After you have played them, you can make up new lists of your own, or have someone else do so. With half a dozen players in the game, each one can make up a list using key-words of his choice; then he acts as the referee while the others play.

Making up lists of Type A ("End Each Word") is quite simple, as you can take them in order from a dictionary, including the definition with each key-syllable. Type B ("Middle of the Worders") will require a lot more ingenuity. Type C ("Begin Each Word") can prove quite tough, unless you hit on a "happy ending" which offers a lot of choices. Type D ("Zigzags") is the most difficult, but worth the effort if you hit a neat "key-word."

In any case, making your own lists is an especially good exercise in word recognition and therefore very helpful experience toward reading to remember.

END EACH WORD

Supply the necessary letters to end each word according to the definitions that accompany it.

1. C A L _ _ _	Immature
2. C A L _ _ _	An oriental ruler
3. C A L _ _ _	A man's name
4. C A L _ _ _	A cotton cloth
5. C A L _ _ _	Young animals
6. C A L _ _ _	A visitor
7. C A L _ _ _ _	A measuring instrument
8. C A L _ _ _ _	A silver-white metal
9. C A L _ _ _ _	Degree of excellence
10. C A L _ _ _ _	Pertaining to diet
11. C A L _ _ _ _ _	Misfortune or catastrophe
12. C A L _ _ _ _ _	Something used the year around
13. C A L _ _ _ _ _	A kind of gourd
14. C A L _ _ _ _ _ _	To reckon or compute
15. C A L _ _ _ _ _ _ _	A state

MIDDLE OF THE WORDERS

With each word, add the necessary letters *before and after* to form a complete word fitting the definition given with it.

1. _ _ E A T _ _   Swindled
2. _ _ E A T _ _   Something bigger
3. _ _ E A T _ _   Simply to live
4. _ _ E A T _ _   A popular garment
5. _ _ E A T _ _   Maker
6. _ _ E A T _ _   Folded in special fashion

7. _ _ A R T _ _   An ancient Greek
8. _ _ A R T _ _   Surprise or frighten
9. _ _ A R T _ _   A special grant or privilege
10. _ _ A R T _ _   Began
11. _ _ A R T _ _   Of dark complexion
12. _ _ A R T _ _   Give or gain courage

BEGIN EACH WORD

Try to fill in the beginning of each word to reach the TRY that completes it! Each blank represents a needed letter and the full word must fit the definition that follows it.

1. _ _ _ T R Y   Rhyme and verse
2. _ _ _ T R Y   Hot and close
3. _ _ _ T R Y   A tasty dessert
4. _ _ _ T R Y   Soldier on guard
5. _ _ _ T R Y   A part of a church
6. _ _ _ T R Y   Cold and bleak
7. _ _ _ T R Y   A serving room
8. _ _ _ T R Y   Class of landowners
9. _ _ _ T R Y   Small or worthless

10. _ _ _ _ _ T R Y   Soldiers on the march
11. _ _ _ _ _ T R Y   Harmonious proportion
12. _ _ _ _ _ T R Y   A branch of mathematics
13. _ _ _ _ _ T R Y   Pedigree or lineage
14. _ _ _ _ _ T R Y   Ornamental woven cloth
15. _ _ _ _ _ T R Y   An official recording

ZIGZAG WORDS

In these groups, the key combinations HER, TON, BAN, ONE, occupy different positions in each word. As a result, some of the full words may be tricky when you form them from the definitions.

1.	H E R _ _ _	A drug
2.	_ H E R _ _	A fruit
3.	_ _ H E R _	A globe
4.	_ _ _ H E R	A parent
5.	_ _ _ _ T O N	An American city, capital of its state
6.	_ _ T O N _	Ornamental staffs
7.	_ T O N _ _	Made amends
8.	T O N _ _ _	A term for language
9.	B A N _ _ _	Good-humored ridicule
10.	_ B A N _ _	Noted Spanish author
11.	_ _ B A N _	A capital of a state
12.	_ _ _ B A N	A type of headgear
13.	_ _ _ O N E	Belonging to the past
14.	_ _ O N E _	Scottish cakes
15.	_ O N E _ _	Straightforward
16.	O N E _ _ _	A lake in New York State named after an Indian tribe

ANSWERS TO KEY-WORDS

(*a*) *End of Each Word*

1. CALLOW 2. CALIPH 3. CALVIN 4. CALICO 5. CALVES 6. CALLER
7. CALIPER 8. CALCIUM 9. CALIBER 10. CALORIE
11. CALAMITY 12. CALENDAR 13. CALABASH
14. CALCULATE 15. CALIFORNIA

(*b*) *Middle of the Worders*

1. CHEATED 2. GREATER 3. BREATHE 4. SWEATER
5. CREATOR 6. PLEATED 7. SPARTAN 8. STARTLE 9. CHARTER
10. STARTED 11. SWARTHY 12. HEARTEN

(*c*) *Begin Each Word*

1. POETRY 2. SULTRY 3. PASTRY 4. SENTRY 5. VESTRY
6. WINTRY 7. PANTRY 8. GENTRY 9. PALTRY 10. INFANTRY
11. SYMMETRY 12. GEOMETRY 13. ANCESTRY 14. TAPESTRY
15. REGISTRY

(*d*) *Zigzag Words*

1. HEROIN 2. CHERRY 3. SPHERE 4. FATHER
5. BOSTON 6. BATONS 7. ATONE 8. TONGUE
9. BANTER 10. IBANEZ 11. ALBANY 12. TURBAN
13. BYGONE 14. SCONES 15. HONEST 16. ONEIDA

THE GAME OF GHOSTS

Though old and well known, this is one of the best word games, as it demands considerable knowledge of words and their formation. Often, a player must picture words well ahead in order to win. The game, in a sense, is always new, as increases in modern terminology have made it much more competitive than it once was. However, it also has the advantage of being suitable to all ages, as younger players, with more limited vocabularies, may find the contest even keener than their more erudite elders.

The game can be played verbally, or with paper and pencil, but the latter course is recommended as it allows checking back and also stresses the actual formation of the words. This is of value in increasing writing and reading vocabularies as well as the spoken and overall vocabularies. Hence the game will prove helpful in reading to remember.

Any number of persons may play, up to a half a dozen. As an illustration, let us take a game with five participants, *A,B,C,D,E*. The game is begun by *A*, who names any letter of the alphabet, say the letter *T*. Player *B* then adds another letter, but it must go toward the formation of a word. If *B* should say *G*, the letters *TG* would be meaningless. The next player, *C* could challenge *B*, asking what word he had in mind. Having none, *B* would lose, and thus have one point against him.

Naturally, *B* would give a more sensible letter than G. He could say O, as there are many words with the beginning T-O. But right here, we must insert a warning. Though each letter goes toward the forming of an ultimate word, any player completing an actual word, ends the round and loses, a point being charged against him. Accordingly, he must avoid completing words himself, pushing that burden on to someone else.

However, this does not apply with two-letter words, so *B* is quite safe in making it T-O. This is customary in the early stages, as many two-letter words, like AM, IS, GO, PA, etc., are necessary starters for longer words. *B* could have said H, making it T-H, which is a good starter, though not a word; but let us assume he made it T-O.

Now, it is up to *C*. He immediately thinks of the letter M. Nicknames do not count in this game, so they are safe to use. but only at times! This is one time when to add an M and form the nickname TOM would be a mistake. That is because TOM is also an actual word, meaning the male of a species. Such being the case, *C* very smartly avoids M. Starting through the alphabet, he hits the letter B and does some quick calculation.

The letters TOB can be built into the word TOBACCO. *C* is the third player; counting ahead, he pictures the fourth player making it TOBA; the fifth player, TOBAC; the first player, TOBACC; the second player, TOBACCO. In short, going the rounds, it will wind up with Player *B* forming the finished word and becoming the loser, before it even gets to Player *C*. As a result, Player *C* makes it T-O-B.

But the next player *D*, doesn't happen to think of TOBACCO. The word that comes first to his mind is TOBOGGAN, and he figures it is safe enough for him. So he makes it T-O-B-O.

Player *E* has to go along with TOBOGGAN, so he makes it T-O-B-O-G; Player *A* makes it T-O-B-O-G-G; Player *B* goes to T-O-B-O-G-G-A; and Player *C* has to make it T-O-B-O-G-G-A-N, hitting a real toboggan slide and losing on what he thought would be a safe choice with TOBACCO instead of TOBOGGAN.

It would look as though players are sometimes sure to be crushed by an inevitable word of the toboggan type, but that is not always so. Suppose that Player *E* had failed to think of the word TOBOGGAN. He could very well have decided that Player *D* was bluffing with his T-O-B-O, and that there was no word with such a beginning. Then *E* would have challenged *D* to name the word he had in mind. When *D* named TOBOGGAN, the round would end with *E* as the loser, because his challenge failed. Player *C* would be saved, because the word would not come around to him.

Where do the "ghosts" come in? In the following way: After

a player has lost three times, he becomes a "ghost" and drops from play. One loss makes him, "one-third of a ghost," two losses, "two-thirds of a ghost" and three, a ghost itself. This continues until all players but one have been eliminated; that player then becomes a winner.

In a juvenile form of the game, the eliminated players are allowed to talk to the other players, but the others can not talk to them. Anyone who does, becomes a "ghost" himself and by an extension of this rule, his place is taken by the person to whom he spoke. Such opportunities are frequent, as a "ghost" can ask players why they chose certain letters, or if they are ready to be challenged. Often, a player may reply unthinkingly to such a question.

However, in more advanced play, the "ghost" factor may be dropped entirely. Nobody is eliminated. Player *A* starts a word, and whoever finishes it has a point scored against him. Player *B* then starts a word and again a point is scored against the finisher. Remaining players begin words in order and this goes on until a specified number of rounds have been completed. Then, the player with the lowest score—the fewest counts against him—is the winner.

THE PALINDROME GAME

The term "palindrome" applies to words or sentences which read the same backward and forward. There are many such words in the English language, as EVE, NOON, CIVIC, and even the coined word RADAR. Noting such words can be useful for reading and remembering, and it may be developed into a game as well.

True palindromes can be more than reversible words; they may be whole sentences that can be read back and forth. Most noted of these is the Latin phrase:

SATOR   AREPO   TENET   OPERA   ROTAS

These words, incidentally, form a word square in which each

word can be read from left to right, right to left; top to bottom, and
bottom to top:

S A T O R

A R E P O

T E N E T

O P E R A

R O T A S

In English, there is a famous palindrome that stands as a
perfect example of a word-by-word sentence that can be read both
ways. It is a remark that could have been made by Napoleon:

"ABLE WAS I ERE I SAW ELBA."

Another perfect English palindrome is the phrase:

"REPEL EVIL A LIVE LEPER"

Others have been devised that are not quite perfect, because
the word letters must be regrouped when read in reverse. An appropriate Latin phrase runs:

"ROMA IBI TIBI SEDES IBI TIBI AMOR"

The "ibi tibi" must be broken differently when spelled backward, but the letters are all in proper order. The phrase can be
translated, "At Rome you live, at Rome you love."

An example of a slightly imperfect English palindrome is the
mournful summer cry of the owl:

"TOO HOT TO HOOT"

And further, there is the comment by a fussy gentleman:

"EGAD A BASE TONE DENOTES A BAD AGE"

Most renowned, very likely, of all English palindromes is the
remark that Adam said when he introduced himself to Eve:

"MADAM, I'M ADAM"

Now, in the game of Palindromes that we are about to de-
scribe, there is no need to form full palindrome phrases, either
perfect or imperfect. Instead, the game is simply to pair up words
that together form a palindrome, as PIN—NIP, or MEET—TEEM.

As clues to such words, they are given as gaps in sentences. Copies of this should be made and supplied to various players.

A suitable list follows:

1. While traveling through Oklahoma, we stopped to _ _ _ _ in the town of _ _ _ _ _.
2. At the approach of _ _ _ _ _, he adopted a solemn _ _ _ _.
3. Pythias felt that his friend _ _ _ _ _ _ was something of a wandering _ _ _ _ _.
4. Drinking too much _ _ _   _ _ _ can drive a man to _ _ _ _ _ _.
5. He attracted the _ _ _ _ _ by a piping note played on a hollow _ _ _ _.
6. He had to _ _ _ _ _ the shipping news before the _ _ _ _ went out.
7. I like cheese that is _ _ _ _ _ in _ _ _ _ _.
8. He _ _ _ _ _ the coin on the _ _ _ _ _ of the watch.
9. They found a nice _ _ _ _ _ to spin their _ _ _ _ _.
10. He found the _ _ _ _ _ _ _ money in the top _ _ _ _ _ _.
11. The fox ran away with _ _ _ _ _ of the _ _ _ _ _.
12. The acrobat did a _ _ _ _ _ as he dived into the _ _ _ _ _.
13. When playing _ _ _ _ _, never try to _ _ _ _ _ the ball.
14. The window of the _ _ _ _ _ looked out over the _ _ _ _.
15. The horses pulled the _ _ _ _ _ out of the _ _ _ _ _.
16. You should _ _ _ _ _ a man who has a _ _ _ _ _ goal.

In number 4, the first space is composed of two words—as indicated by the separation—and the second space is a single word in which the order of the letters is reversed.

In playing this game, whoever fills the most words within a set time limit is the winner. New lists of palindrome words can be prepared for other games. That is quite a task in itself, so it can be turned into a game too.

Simply have several players think up words that become other words when turned about. Whoever composes the longest list within fifteen minutes is the winner.

ANSWERS TO THE PALINDROME GAME

1. DINE—ENID
2. DOOM—MOOD
3. DAMON—NOMAD
4. RED RUM—MURDER
5. DEER—REED
6. EDIT—TIDE
7. MADE—EDAM
8. LAID—DIAL
9. SPOT—TOPS
10. REWARD—DRAWER
11. PART—TRAP
12. LOOP—POOL
13. GOLF—FLOG
14. ROOM—MOOR
15. DRAY—YARD
16. LAUD—DUAL

Each pair of words or terms is spelled with the same letters in reverse.

THE ANAGRAM GAME

Two words composed of the same letters, differently arranged, are known as anagrams. Formations of this type have been used in many games. The simplest type is merely a "word scramble" in which the letters of a word are mixed and the object is to put them in their proper order.

Other such games consist of making two or more words out of jumbled letters; but in the true sense, the changing of one word to another, by rearranging the letters, constitutes an anagram process. The only questions are these: With which word should you begin? And what should you do if there is more than one possible answer?

Both of those questions are answered in the game that follows. Instead of jumbling letters, or giving one word outright, the components of the anagram have been placed as spaces in a sentence, which in itself helps toward guessing the missing words. Hence, in each sentence that follows, the missing words are spelled with the same letters differently arranged.

Go through the list to see how fast you can supply the needed words; or supply identical lists to various players and let each try to finish first:

1. The king _ _ _ _ _ an order releasing the prisoner from the _ _ _ _ _.
2. The more he _ _ _ _ _ _, the _ _ _ _ _ _ his temper became.
3. The jewelers were _ _ _ _ _ _ _ than ever, setting _ _ _ _ _ _ in gold rings.
4. Did you ever _ _ _ _ _ bread with the _ _ _ _ _ who made it?
5. In a winter storm, a driving _ _ _ _ _ _ can cut like bits of _ _ _ _ _ _.
6. Sometimes, at big _ _ _ _ _ _, the crowd _ _ _ _ _ _ _ the horses.
7. The landlord filled the flowing _ _ _ _ _ until the _ _ _ _ _ ran over.
8. When the barnyard is in _ _ _ _ _ _ _ _, a big _ _ _ _ _ _ will often honk a warning.
9. He rode his _ _ _ _ _ _ along the ocean's _ _ _ _ _ _ _.
10. We will be _ _ _ _ _ _ at _ _ _ _ _ _ o'clock.
11. In many games, after one player _ _ _ _ _ _, the man on his left _ _ _ _ _ _ a card.
12. In poetry, only a special word may _ _ _ _ _ _, to complete a _ _ _ _ _ _.
13. It is great _ _ _ _ _ _ to sail for unknown _ _ _ _ _ _.
14. Before eating a _ _ _ _ _, you should _ _ _ _ it with a knife.
15. The _ _ _ _ _ _ of five colleges held a meeting high in the _ _ _ _ _ _ Mountains.
16. A _ _ _ _ _ _ lamp may hurt your eyes because of its strong _ _ _ _ _ _.

It is comparatively easy to prepare new lists of Anagram Words, and that can be made into a game of its own, with a time limit to see which player can come up with the most. Then, those words can be worked into sentences, so that other persons can play the Anagram Game as already given.

This works out exactly as with Palindromes, but forming Anagrams is easier. Actually, a palindrome is also an anagram, but of a specialized type. That's why it is easier to make up anagrams.

ANSWERS TO THE ANAGRAM GAME

1. WROTE—TOWER
2. SWORE—WORSE
3. BUSIER—RUBIES
4. BREAK—BAKER
5. SLEET—STEEL
6. RACES—SCARE
7. POTS—TOPS
8. DANGER—GANDER
9. HORSE—SHORE
10. THERE—THREE
11. DEALS—LEADS
12. SERVE—VERSE
13. SPORT—PORTS
14. PEAR—PARE
15. DEANS—ANDES
16. LARGE—GLARE

Each pair of words is spelled with exactly the same letters, differently arranged.

How
to speed
comprehension
and

XI   increase

retention

The paired factors of Speed of Comprehension and
Ratio of Retention are the twofold goal of Reading to
Remember. How one can be geared to the other, becomes
the subject of immediate importance.

Check-backs and tests are applied to Reading to Remember, showing how speed can be gauged in relation of
material. Typograhy and other factors are also important.

The "fog index" enters as a reading factor. "Fogging"
and its management are considered through practical approaches. Further tests with the Read-O-dometer are utilized
as applicable.

All these are bolstering steps toward turning reading
skill into an art, which is compared with other forms of
artistic achievement. As with the various arts, reading improvement can be gained through continued application.

Two factors summarize our efforts in reading to remember:
Speed of Comprehension and Ratio of Retention.

As you read faster you must comprehend accordingly, or
sufficiently to maintain the pace. Similarly, the amount you remember must be proportional to your newly acquired speed. When

you read twice as fast but remember only the same amount as you did before, you have accomplished nothing. Even worse, if you read faster and remember less, you are defeating your basic purpose. Hence the twin factors of reading and remembering should be balanced, so to speak. However, the two processes, though closely interrelated, can be improved independently in many ways. If your faster reading gets you nowhere, spend some time on memory methods and vice versa.

Avoidance of Extremes
in Reading to Remember

There have been cases of persons who have been painstaking with everything they have read, remembering practically every detail. These people have become exacting in their way, acquiring wonderful memory stores that have won them acclaim from their friends, occasionally from the public at large. Some have even developed into memory experts. Usually, their scope of knowledge has been so limited or so confined to facts and statistics, that they have accomplished little beyond their own restricted spheres.

In contrast, there are avid readers who rush rapidly from one book to another while they almost completely forget the things that they have read before. They may still manage to be quite respected in many circles as "well read," because if other people raise questions, they may come up with the answers. That is, they have sufficient literary qualifications to know what other people are talking about if their memories are jogged. But, generally they are unable to accomplish anything on their own, with their minds cluttered by smatterings of knowledge which only echo whatever someone else shouts.

Gearing Speed of Comprehension
to Ratio of Retention

How are you to synchronize those twin assets of reading and remembering? How can speed of comprehension be geared to the ratio of retention? Very practically. By working on each not only jointly but independently, giving both factors the proper amount of attention and recognition. A parallel example is the speed typist, who actually must comprehend each word, each phrase, and each sentence in order to produce efficient results in some situations. Continuous effort at improvement in this one direction can bring greater speed. Now with reading, it is very much the same. The process can be sped through its proper application; the aim, instead of being the material set down on a typewritten page, is the amount of data retained in the mind.

That raises the question: Where is the limit?

In typing, there is a record limit although few people manage to reach it. The rest—experts included—are quite satisfied when they have gained a pace which they know approaches the contest maximum or is fast enough to suit their own purposes. That should be the case with reading as well, though here you can often go far beyond what you might originally think were your limitations. If we pursue the typing analogy further, this becomes quite plain.

The typist's speed is restrained by physical limitations, such as the keyboard of the typewriter and the reaction of the human fingers. If the typist had a keyboard combining letters such as *th, ph,* and better still, simple words like *be, he, the, there,* and many more, the typist's speed might be expected to reach incredible proportions. It would be defeated however, by the complexity of the keyboard; that is the big problem.

Now in reading, that problem does not exist. It is substantially as easy to recognize letter combinations and simple words, as it is to note individual letters; in fact, the faster you read, the more you begin to expand into such phases. By this means, speeding your reading becomes a natural process. There are, however, physical problems too.

These include bad reading habits and bad lighting. Then, perhaps worst of all, there is the inability to recognize when you are reading badly. Here the typist has an advantage, because the work that comes from the typewriter can itself be judged in terms of capability. In reading, the only quick way you have to check back is by retracing what you have remembered. What this amounts to is that you are judging speed of comprehension by ratio of retention. As opposed to typing, the comparison, instead of being merely physical, is mental.

Value of Check-backs and
Tests in Reading to Remember

As your reading skill increases, and you realize that you are reading faster than before, your next step is to check back on a reading period and see how much you remembered. Then continue to improve your reading, and after a due interval, when you know that you are reading still faster than before, pause again to see how your memory process is faring. If you are remembering relatively as much as or more than before, results can be regarded as satisfactory. On the contrary, if the faster reading leads to remembering less, it is time to build up the ratio of retention.

One essential, then, is that you should test yourself or have yourself tested. You should practice on all weak spots and keep building while you keep reading. Your aim is to balance reading speed with memorizing power and at the same time recognize that each has its own separate purpose. Fast reading can be understood without memorization of detail, therefore you should keep up your speed practices. But don't let them stray from the necessity for controlled memorization which is the ultimate aim and the real regulatory factor in more serious reading.

Necessity of Noting Content
and Substance of All You Read

This brings us to the important point that the more complex the material, the slower both the reading and the remembering. We may have given the impression that typing is a mechanical process, but there are certain forms of typing which demand closer attention and can slow the pace, technical stenography being a good example.

Similarly in reading, there are proof readers who make a specialty of going over material and looking for mistakes. This type of reading requires closer attention to detail than ordinary reading would. At the same time, it is interesting to note that specialty typists—such as legal stenographers—may often be correct on all technical details, yet make mistakes in simpler ways.

Correspondingly, a proof reader may mark a final proof as correct, because all the words are properly spelled and the sentence structure is exact, yet the whole meaning of the material may be lost, through some slight error that was overlooked by the proof reader who was reading for exactitude and not for substance.

Hence, you come to realize that in developing your skills of reading and remembering, it is basic to improve the pace yet keep it within reason. The speed must be gauged in the relation of the material, always with the purpose of going faster when feasible, but never to the detriment of the final result.

If, while reading, you feel that you should go slower, do so, but make this part of your proficiency. Good judgment in reading speed is just like good judgment in driving a car or in any other skill. Speed up when you can but slacken when you see the warning signs.

As an example of how reading speed in itself can be affected, you can test yourself with the presentation of the same passage on page 213. In reading one, you will automatically become familiar with the material which appears in the others. Each utilizes a different form of typography. The first is an ordinary bookface type, the next Old English, the next italics, then boldface type, and finally a script. You will find that as you read, your speed will be governed by the type itself.

Examples of Typography Analyzed in Terms of Reading Speed

The Old English presents an unfamiliarity, the italics and boldface shows stress or importance, and the script results in another reading approach. Just exactly how much your speed may vary is not too important here; the main point is the variance itself.

Assume that you read each type paragraph so that your speed of comprehension was the same and resulted in the usual ratio of retention. You will easily see that if you had sped the reading process about equally in all paragraphs, you would have reduced your results. Such obstacles, when met with in reading, can be classed as typographical warnings. But if you customarily read passages in any of the less familiar forms of type or in those that are emphasized, you would soon become accustomed to them and your speed of comprehension and ratio of retention would return to normal.

The "Fog Index" in Reading and the Problems It Predicts

Quite often, you will find that texts set up in standard type can sometimes become as obscure as unfamiliar typography. This occurs when you are confronted with strange technical terms, frequent many syllable words, or very complex sentences. Efforts to continue your usual speed could result in serious loss of comprehension, or "fogging." That term is practically self-explanatory: it refers to a state where comprehension becomes clouded because you are missing too many essential words and their relationships.

Among the most important elements measuring reading ease are sentence length and word difficulty. A method of relating these has been expressed in the creation of a "Fog Index." This provides a yardstick for readability based upon a proportion between hard words and sentence length. Writing that has a higher fog index is understood with more difficulty. For example, the fog index generally increases through the following types of magazines in the order given: Pulp fiction, slick fiction, digests, quality, scientific.

This does not mean that "better writing" will always "fog" inexperienced readers, for some of the finest of all writing has been noted for its simplicity of style. While "fogging" results from encountering too many unusual words or complicated sentences,

Their escutcheons have long mouldered from the walls of their castles. Their castles themselves are but green mounds and shattered ruins—the place that once knew them, knows them no more—nay, many a race since theirs has died out and been forgotten in the very land which they occupied, with all the authority of feudal proprietors and feudal lords.

𝕿𝖍𝖊𝖎𝖗 𝖊𝖘𝖈𝖚𝖙𝖈𝖍𝖊𝖔𝖓𝖘 𝖍𝖆𝖛𝖊 𝖑𝖔𝖓𝖌 𝖒𝖔𝖚𝖑𝖉𝖊𝖗𝖊𝖉 𝖋𝖗𝖔𝖒 𝖙𝖍𝖊 𝖜𝖆𝖑𝖑𝖘 𝖔𝖋 𝖙𝖍𝖊𝖎𝖗 𝖈𝖆𝖘𝖙𝖑𝖊𝖘. 𝕿𝖍𝖊𝖎𝖗 𝖈𝖆𝖘𝖙𝖑𝖊𝖘 𝖙𝖍𝖊𝖒𝖘𝖊𝖑𝖛𝖊𝖘 𝖆𝖗𝖊 𝖇𝖚𝖙 𝖌𝖗𝖊𝖊𝖓 𝖒𝖔𝖚𝖓𝖉𝖘 𝖆𝖓𝖉 𝖘𝖍𝖆𝖙𝖙𝖊𝖗𝖊𝖉 𝖗𝖚𝖎𝖓𝖘—𝖙𝖍𝖊 𝖕𝖑𝖆𝖈𝖊 𝖙𝖍𝖆𝖙 𝖔𝖓𝖈𝖊 𝖐𝖓𝖊𝖜 𝖙𝖍𝖊𝖒, 𝖐𝖓𝖔𝖜𝖘 𝖙𝖍𝖊𝖒 𝖓𝖔 𝖒𝖔𝖗𝖊—𝖓𝖆𝖞, 𝖒𝖆𝖓𝖞 𝖆 𝖗𝖆𝖈𝖊 𝖘𝖎𝖓𝖈𝖊 𝖙𝖍𝖊𝖎𝖗𝖘 𝖍𝖆𝖘 𝖉𝖎𝖊𝖉 𝖔𝖚𝖙 𝖆𝖓𝖉 𝖍𝖆𝖘 𝖇𝖊𝖊𝖓 𝖋𝖔𝖗𝖌𝖔𝖙𝖙𝖊𝖓 𝖎𝖓 𝖙𝖍𝖊 𝖛𝖊𝖗𝖞 𝖑𝖆𝖓𝖉 𝖜𝖍𝖎𝖈𝖍 𝖙𝖍𝖊𝖞 𝖔𝖈𝖈𝖚𝖕𝖎𝖊𝖉, 𝖜𝖎𝖙𝖍 𝖆𝖑𝖑 𝖙𝖍𝖊 𝖆𝖚𝖙𝖍𝖔𝖗𝖎𝖙𝖞 𝖔𝖋 𝖋𝖊𝖚𝖉𝖆𝖑 𝖕𝖗𝖔𝖕𝖗𝖎𝖊𝖙𝖔𝖗𝖘 𝖆𝖓𝖉 𝖋𝖊𝖚𝖉𝖆𝖑 𝖑𝖔𝖗𝖉𝖘.

Their escutcheons have long mouldered from the walls of their castles. Their castles themselves are but green mounds and shattered ruins—the place that once knew them, knows them no more—nay, many a race since theirs has died out and has been forgotten in the very land which they occupied, with all the authority of feudal proprietors and feudal lords.

Their escutcheons have long mouldered from the walls of their castles. Their castles themselves are but green mounds and shattered ruins—the place that once knew them, knows them no more—nay, many a race since theirs has died out and been forgotten in the very land which they occupied, with all the authority of feudal proprietors and feudal lords.

Their escutcheons have long mouldered from the walls of their castles. Their castles themselves are but green mounds and shattered ruins—the place that once knew them, knows them no more—nay, many a race since theirs has died out and been forgotten in the very land which they occupied, with all the authority of feudal proprietors and feudal lords.

it can also develop from fatigue. That in turn may be due to over-strain where more difficult types of reading are concerned. As an enlightened reader, you should be aware of these factors and be ready to take proper precautions against the fogging hazard.

Ways to Avoid "Fogging" While Maintaining Reading Pace

If you find any type of reading becoming too complex, you should immediately reduce your reading speed. That in itself may remedy the situation. If the material immediately becomes easier to comprehend, too much speed was probably the fault.

If you are still doubtful, you should change your reading process in accordance with the suggestions made in earlier chapters. Pause for review; check back on difficult or unknown words. Take time out to analyze the author's style or settle any other questions that may be in your mind. All this is part of your competent reading procedure, directed toward faster and effective reading in the long run. Likewise, it serves to speed comprehension and speed the ratio of retention.

Experienced readers should never become touchy on the "foggy" question. It is better to take the attitude that all reading is a new experience, which in a sense it is. Years ago, it was customary for people to read and reread material that they particularly liked, and as a result they became "well read" in the full sense of the term. Today there is little time for that, but if you read ten articles by the same author, instead of reading one of his articles ten times over, you are gaining an equivalent experience.

Familiarity with the writer's style and purpose will speed your process very much as if you were going over the same ground. Today people have a wealth of opportunity of this sort, that they did not have before where reading was concerned.

Once, qualified writers were so rare that their material had to be weighed and reconsidered. Nowadays, editorials, digests, columns and the like, guide the reader along the same channels, and with vastly more variety of material at his disposal. But this very factor, encouraging an addiction to certain styles of writing, condensations and the like, may cause unfamiliarity with off-trail reading. You just can't expect to make the same time over back roads or an unfamiliar highway, that you would along the regular turnpike or freeway. Even in driving, you encounter fogs and have to go slower, much the same as you would in reading.

Testing Out "Fogging"
Through Unfamiliar Material

"Fogging" is easy to understand, if you try plunging directly into technical material. You will soon realize that it is better first to acquaint yourself with the technical terms. Do that and you will see how much more rapidly the "fog" clears away. Another excellent example of the "fog" problem is found with foreign languages.

Many persons have learned to read a foreign language in classrooms in regular assignments. But that does not always mean that they can pick up a book in that language and read it off just as they would English. On the contrary, the effect is frequently quite surprising. Often they may find themselves missing words and stumbling over phrases because all their reading up to that point usually had been of a selected type, done in short stages as a study assignment.

It is something of an uncomfortable sensation to try reading a foreign language with which you should be familiar, only to find that your shortcomings are piling up on you as you go along. You realize rapidly that unfamiliarity with idioms and lack of vocabulary are two of the difficulties, to say nothing of style or the question of catching the *motif* itself. Moreover, you begin to feel as though you have gone back to an earlier period when your reading ability was poorly developed.

Consequently, if you run into this problem when reading English, you should be quick to recognize it. It should not always be regarded as a reflection on your reading skill, instead, and most likely being due to your unfamiliarity with certain items. If you are unable to follow the deep discussions of a writer with a mind like Einstein's, you at least have this consolation; that the writer himself might be just as completely "fogged" if he tried to read slang phrases or jive talk.

Comparisons of Full Width and Double Column Pages: Read-O-dometer Review

Assuming that you are quite familiar with certain material and its nomenclature, there are still factors that require different reading paces, with "fogging" always a danger if you try to overdo them. We have already examined differences in typography. Similarly, we can now set guides to the overall appearance of the printed page. Material printed in newspaper columns, or in narrow column "digest" form is usually suited for more rapid reading than the full width book style page.

On page 218, you will see an example of the same material set in two different ways; one as a *full length* line book page, the other in two column digest style. In comparing these, you will note how the eye goes across the full width of the page, picking key words and utilizing the back sweep; whereas with the digest style, the eye can zigzag down each column picking key words in successive lines. Here, you can test this with the Read-O-dometer, finding out for yourself just how much more rapidly you can read the digest style of material. In fact, anytime that you are trying to speed your reading or make it more efficient, you should consider using the Read-O-dometer, as it can be a valuable accessory. This applies to all types of reading matter.

For a further illustration, we are including another page which shows a comparison of identical material in full page width, and in two column style. In this case, the key-words are underlined so that you can see quite plainly how the cross motion and the backsweeps function with the full width page as contrasted to the zigzag reading down the digest column. This is a most important reason why digest material must be specially chosen or carefully condensed. If the sentences are too long and cumbersome, or if hyphenated words appear in the wrong places, it will be defeating its very purpose. With that, it can change a regular rhythm done in consistent zigzags, into jerky and sometimes interrupted downward progress.

How Type Styles Can Speed
Reading Comprehension

There have been cases where heavy novels or other weighty texts have been set in two column digest style, with the mistaken notion that the reader would be aided. Instead, this has only served to make his reading that much harder. Similarly, stories serialized in newspapers can be very difficult to read because of the narrow column, which makes no allowance for the reader's needs in relation to a difficult text. Indeed, it would not be surprising to find that novels were frequently run in thirty or more installments in daily newspapers, because the average reader would literally find himself worn out by the time he reached the end of even a brief installment, due to the fault of the typography.

While the failing in such "horrible examples" are self-evident, there are many other instances where the defects are not quite so apparent. This in a way makes them all the more dangerous, because you can read for a long time without realizing that your speed has been gradually slowing or that the material itself has been losing interest.

You may even feel that your comprehension is below par or that you are "fogging" somewhat, whereas the blame is not your reading ability or lack of same, but may be due entirely to the typography.

Samples of Varied Type
Styles, Comparing Readability

On page 221 you are given three examples of the same material set in full page width but in three different ways. In the

The "flush times" held bravely on. Something over two years before, Mr. Goodman and another journeyman printer had borrowed forty dollars and set out from San Francisco to try their fortunes in the new city of Virginia. They found the *Territorial Enterprise,* a poverty-stricken weekly journal, gasping for breath and likely to die. They bought it, type, fixtures, good-will and all, for a thousand dollars, on long time. The editorial sanctum, news-room, press-room, publication office, bed-chamber, parlor and kitchen were all compressed into one apartment, and it was a small one, too. The editors and printers slept on the floor, a Chinaman did their cooking, and the "imposing stone" was the general dinner-table. But now things were changed. The paper was a great daily, printed by steam; there were five editors and twenty-three compositors; the subscription price was sixteen dollars a year; the advertising rates were exorbitant, and the columns crowded.

The "flush times" held bravely on. Something over two years before, Mr. Goodman and another journeyman printer had borrowed forty dollars and set out from San Francisco to try their fortunes in the new city of Virginia. They found the *Territorial Enterprise,* a poverty-stricken weekly journal, gasping for breath and likely to die. They bought it, type, fixtures, good-will and all, for a thousand dollars, on long time. The editorial sanctum, news-room, press-room, publication office, bed-chamber, parlor and kitchen were all compressed into one apartment, and it was a small one, too. The editors and printers slept on the floor, a Chinaman did their cooking and the "imposing stone" was the general dinner-table. But now things were changed. The paper was a great daily, printed by steam; there were five editors and twenty-three compositors; the subscription price was sixteen dollars a year; the advertising rates were exorbitant, and the columns crowded.

There were nabobs in those days—in the "flush times," I mean. Every rich strike in the mines created one or two. I call to mind several of these. They were careless, easy-going fellows, as a general thing, and the community at large was as much benefitted by their riches as they were themselves —possibly more, in some cases.

Two cousins, teamsters, did some hauling for a man, and had to take a small segregated portion of a silver-mine in lieu of three hundred dollars cash. They gave an outsider a third to open the mine, and they went on teaming. But not long. Ten months afterwards, the mine was out of debt and paying each owner eight to ten thousand dollars a month—say, one hundred thousand dollars a year.

One of the earliest nabobs that Nevada was delivered of wore six thousand dollars' worth of diamonds in his bosom and swore he was unhappy because he could not spend his money as fast as he made it.

There were nabobs in those days—in the "flush times," I mean. Every rich strike in the mines created one or two. I call to mind several of these. They were careless, easy-going fellows, as a general thing, and the community at large was as much benefitted by their riches as they were themselves—possibly more, in some cases.

Two cousins, teamsters, did some hauling for a man, and had to take a small, segregated portion of a silver-mine in lieu of three hundred dollars cash. They gave an outsider a third to open the mine, and they went on teaming. But not long. Ten months afterwards, the mine was out of debt and paying each owner eight to ten thousand dollars a month—say, one hundred thousand dollars a year.

One of the earliest nabobs that Nevada was delivered of wore six thousand dollars' worth of diamonds in his bosom and swore he was unhappy because he could not spend his money as fast as he made it.

first case, the type is ample and extremely readable. The second case shows the same material but reduced in type size to fit a narrower page. This is quite deceptive, because there is actually less eye motion and a shorter backsweep, so the material in a way would seem to be more readable and might even have this effect at the outset. But in the case of prolonged reading, the smaller type can produce a crowding effect and become more tiring to the eye.

With sample A the eye will quickly accomodate itself to the long comfortable lines, as well as the backsweeps. Thus, the longer you read, the easier it may seem to become, with the reading sometimes being prolonged just because of that very factor.

But with sample B, the reading is never really comfortable, becoming more apparent through an earlier lagging of interest and attention. Cramped reading may be likened to a pair of tight shoes; you don't mind them until you try to walk in them, and the longer you walk in them the more they trouble you.

Sample C illustrates the same problem, but in a slightly different way. Here the larger page is used but the type is smaller, putting more words on each line. This requires more pauses and a longer backsweep in each case. It also has the same cramped effect as with the smaller page because the type is set in the same small size.

This reading problem can be met in two ways. In reading material of a classical or informative nature, you frequently have the choice of different texts. If you plan to do extensive reading, pick the text that has the best reading format. It is just that simple, but in many cases you will be astonished to find what a difference it makes. You may also be surprised to discover how often you may have a choice in modern texts.

Great advances in typography have been made in recent years and you will find that the newer editions of many books are much more readable than the old. Unfortunately, the reproduction of hard cover books in cheaper paperback form has often resulted in a hardship on the reader. This is illustrated by comparison of

A.

The former target was now removed, and a fresh one of the same size placed in its room. Hubert, who as victor in the first trial of skill, had the right to shoot first, took aim with great deliberation, long measuring the distance with his eye, while he held in his hand his bended bow, with the arrow placed on the string.

B.

The former target was now removed, and a fresh one of the same size placed in its room. Hubert, who as victor in the first trial of skill, had the right to shoot first, took aim with great deliberation, long measuring the distance with his eye, while he held in his hand his bended bow, with the arrow placed on the string.

C.

The former target was now removed, and a fresh one of the same size placed in its room. Hubert, who as victor in the first trial of skill, had the right to shoot first, took aim with great deliberation, long measuring the distance with his eye, while he held in his hand his bended bow, with the arrow placed on the string.

samples A and B, the first representing standard hard cover text and the second, the typography necessary to bring the material within the range of the usual paperback format.

A comparison of samples A and C shows another form of economy, in the use of smaller type to reduce the number of pages and thereby save costs on paper. This was common in some "Wartime Editions" of books that were published at a time when saving paper was a necessity. Many books are still around that carry the words "Wartime Edition," and this should be a caution that their readability is likely to be of a kind acceptable only during wartime.

Choice of Typography
Toward Sustained Reading

Though some paperback books are being published in the same typography as the standard edition, a majority bow to the factor of economy at the expense of readability. Be aware of this factor and give it due consideration where reading is concerned. You must recognize that both reading speed and endurance can be affected by cramped typography just as they can be handicapped by poor lighting or uncomfortable surroundings or by your own mood or physical condition. A necessary step then, is to check the type before starting and gear your reading accordingly. Don't try too hard to read fast or long if the type presents problems.

The advances of clarity in type have sometimes caused publishers to boobytrap themselves where readers are concerned. One illustration of this is worthy of note because it has a direct bearing on the subject of readability as we are now discussing it. Some years back, due to demands of a rapidly expanding modern terminology and increases in technical terms, dictionaries favored thinner paper more and more to keep them within reasonable size. When that did not suffice, type size was reduced in many. Despite this, the lexicons were still found quite as satisfactory for the average consultant.

Meanwhile, encyclopedias were having the same problem on a larger scale. They went to thinner paper, and also reduced the type size, very likely on the theory that what went for dictionaries would go for encyclopedias. Instead, the result was distressing. Readers who could skip from word to word picking up a few dozen dictionary definitions in rapid order, often bogged down almost completely when they tried to quickly assimilate a single article from a page of the similarly designed encyclopedia. The reason was that for many, sustained reading was impossible with such small type; that is, impossible without the reader showing very early signs of wear and tear.

This factor can be related to ordinary reading as well. You become faced with the situation of how soon an inadequate type size can begin to wear you down; or putting it conversely, how long you can stand up under the strain.

This, and all the various issues discussed in this chapter bring home the point that you should give to the perfection of your reading ability the same attention and respect that you would devote to the cultivation of any other skill. An accomplished orator, actor or musician takes a distinct pride in his work or achievement. The same applies to reading, for a good reader can also derive an intense satisfaction from proficiency.

Steps Toward Turning
Reading Skill Into an Art

The more attention you devote to reading, the more it becomes an art. The more attention you devote to any art, the more capable you can become at it. What we have tried to do throughout this book has been to increase your artistic ability where reading is concerned. No art is ever acquired through rapid, sudden steps, but only with continued sustained effort and practice. As with any art, reading allows for constant practice. Think of anything else you want: music, dancing, painting, sculpture. All those require concentrated effort with a devotion to the subject.

You can easily see the progress that you are making in those fields, and you may relate it directly to the attention applied. With reading, this is not noticed as it is part of the normal routine. Whatever progress you make, you discover afterward, if you compare the earlier results with the later. Few people do that. They simply feel that their reading improves as their age advances; that it is all part of a natural growth, but this is not really the case.

A study of other arts and skills, such as music, chess, knowledge of foreign languages, will reveal to you that there have been child prodigies who excelled in those things at a fantastically early age. Many of these were skilled in reading too, but that came to be regarded as simply part of the remarkable abilities of such geniuses. Yet, actually the acquisition of the reading skill was just as much an achievement as any of the others. Supporting this view are the cases of prodigies in mathematics and other fields who were practically illiterate.

Reading, like speech, is something that can be generally acquired by the majority of the public at large. Yet even with speech, a great orator like Daniel Webster, becomes recognized as a genius in his own right. The same type of distinction should apply to skilled and advanced reading, though this is seldom appreciated. As an art, reading can lay claim to being among the greatest, perhaps the foremost, since it has such universal appeal, and can become a part of almost everyone's ability.

How to maintain
your
effectivness
when
XII   reading
to remember

In summarizing all that we have covered, we can begin from the important premise that reading itself is a matter of remembering; and that memory is essential to improve your reading. This dual concept goes still further; unless you remember some portion of what you read, there is not much purpose in reading at all. You have also found that certain basic factors which are essential to remembering are also essential to reading, namely: interest, attention and repetition. Those add up to association which is the vital key of memory.

You have become more aware of how reading leads to learning, through memory of facts and evaluation. The observation that reading facility increases with learning has emphasized memory as a key or common factor.

Reasons for Reading, and Improvement of Conditions

Your reasons for reading should be kept in mind continually. Their variety and goals have been covered in early chapters of this book. You may read for recreation, for occupational purposes, for acquisition of facts, research, or self-development. All these require different reading speeds which have been discussed throughout the volume. All can be improved by intelligently controlled faster reading, which speeds memory processes, increases familiarity with words and facility in reading them. Hence, speed and memorization can both be increased through proper synchronization.

All these points are directed toward persons who already have some degree of reading skill. One factor they tend to overlook which can produce more efficient reading is environment. Many persons who are already capable readers, may also be stifling their own development through bad reading habits and neglect of proper reading conditions.

Improvement of reading conditions invariably promotes improvement of reading itself. Actually, you must have good reading conditions in order to help overcome certain bad reading habits, otherwise, you may not be so readily aware of such faults. Bad eye habits such as too many pauses, irregular progressions, and other faults including regressions in reading have been brought to attention in earlier chapters, and should be remembered as to their disadvantages even later.

At the same time, such treacherous habits as vocalization, finger pointing, skipping and regressions, must be recognized as occasionally useful steps toward memorization. Therefore, their elimination should be undertaken with due care so as not to lose any of the ability which they may have helped to sustain. In short, we creep before we walk and we walk before we run. If we had been using crutches, we do not throw them away until we are sure that we can get along without them.

Sometimes very good readers have a number of these very bad reading habits. It is not always wise to go back to mere preliminaries and basic training in order to correct them. If you keep improving the assets that you have, there will be less room for liabilities, so that discarding them is simplified. Thus, you can manage with greater ease to move from a clumsier form of reading to the more efficient type which nurtures automatic memorization and is more truly reading to remember.

Reviewing Memory Methods
as Applied to Reading

Reading habits in themselves may serve as memory jogs. An understanding of these and of their occasional application with the different speeds of reading has been covered. All through the process of development of more efficient reading and remembering, the use of the Read-O-dometer was explained and frequently encouraged. An awareness of this device and its purpose, incidentally, should be considered of value and importance through the entire study of reading improvement.

Ways were constantly stressed whereby reading can be keyed to remembering. Among these, visualization or the mental transcribing of words to actions was emphasized as an important adjunct. Memory links through association of words and ideas, was treated as a special subject in itself, for the further this is developed, the greater is the opportunity for expansion of the reading proficiency.

Samples of reducing entire phrases to single words were also given as means for greatly speeding reading. Thereby, phrases can be effectively pictured.

Vocabulary Extension Through
Word-Building Studies

Word building was cited as a method of vocabulary expansion. This leads to the need for your detailed acquaintanceship with prefixes and suffixes, along with the spotting of "words within words" as reading speeders. Here, when using the Read-O-dometer, observation is made of "sight-words" from which others can be rapidly built. The use of flash cards with a quick-view window or method, was explained as a simple device resembling, and at least supplementing the more elaborate tachistoscopic aids. A list of selected flash words again introduced the game angle.

Throughout the earlier chapters, all details regarding how to

read faster and remember more were directed toward a synchoniz-
ing or balancing of those two factors. Attaining this dual goal
hinged upon four types of reading: pleasure, cultural, informative,
and self-improvement. The first three were examined together in
detail, to show how reading speeds should be managed in each
case. After inquiring into the overall principles, an understanding
was obtained of the fourth type of reading, namely self-improvement.

Self-Improvement Through Reading
Techniques and Simple Mnemonics

Reading for self-improvement, which included all of the types
previously listed, was epitomized in four steps: *S*election, *E*xpan-
sion, *L*earning, *F*inishing, thus forming the key-word SELF. This
was followed by a description and elucidation of some of the more
highly developed general reading techniques in favor today: The
Five S Method, the RTP Formula, the PERU System, the PQRST
Formula, and the SQ3R or Survey Q3R. These were designed to
speed reading and increase memorization through natural processes,
but they also serve as study methods. From them, we were able to
move directly into artificial memory systems and their timely em-
ployment, where faster and more efficient reading is concerned.

The use of simple mnemonics was presented together with
devices such as acronyms, acrostics and the like. Then, an ancient
artificial memory aid, the topical or "Room System" as it came
to be known, was carefully explored. This included familiarization
with its use and its extension, with further examples incorporating
its utility in the memorization of poetry.

Next, the "Chain System" was described as another effective
artificial memory device, either as alternate for the Room System,
or for purposes to which the Chain System is more adaptable.
Examples of the "linkage" featuring the Chain System, were shown,
with suggestions as to its expanding use.

Importance of the Figure
Alphabet and Alternate Memory Aids

The most effective and elaborately developed of all artificial memory devices, the "Figure Alphabet" was characterized as a subject in its own right. This device serves a very specific purpose of aiding the user to remember dates, facts and figures in the course of regular reading, often with only slight interruption. It forms a superior adjunct toward any effort to read faster and remember more.

Along with the ten basic figures and their phonetic equivalents, you were given examples of how to use the Figure Alphabet. Then, the list was extended to include 20 to 100 key-words, so the system could be expanded according to individual needs. More examples were cited showing the flexibility and adaptability of the Figure Alphabet.

For completeness, alternates were given in the form of other systems, which though lacking the scope of the Figure Alphabet, serve a similar purpose to a limited extent.

Following this, a section on Memory Games appears, designed for testing many of the factors learned in regard to reading and remembering, and as profitable for activation of memory. These games are governed by patterns suggested in the earlier chapters, in themselves a token of their value. The games can be used repeatedly as word builders and toward the expansion of vocabulary, both precious assets toward reading faster and remembering more.

The Twofold Goal: Speed of
Comprehension and Ratio of Retention

All the factors of reading faster and remembering more were finally summed under the twofold goal of "Speed of Comprehension" and "Ratio of Retention." Once that has been geared properly, you can pace your reading according to the material at hand. Warning was given as to handicaps arising from a high "fog index" where comprehension suffers not just from cumbersome and intricate sentences, but from "hard" words or a lack of familiarity with the subject matter. Guidance for avoiding this was supplied, after an analysis of fogging and its causes. Samples of typography helped elucidation of the points.

Throughout the book, it has been apparent that reading becomes a continued development with the average reader. Hence, with his constantly increasing skill, he should become selective in his reading. Just as you progress in other subjects, so does your reading scope improve. Though increased speed may not be too apparent, often you may actually be reading relatively much faster, because of the longer words and more complex phrases you are taking in with the same stride as you used for the shorter words and simpler material.

Assays of Reading and Remembering: Restoring Dormant Memory

This, in turn, shows that you are remembering more, as the recognition of newer and less familiar words makes that a self-evident fact. Continued application to reading builds more speed, which in turn demands more memory. It becomes a case of giving each due attention to keep the two in harmony. Merely trying to speed your reading is not enough; nor is it wise to strain in order to remember more. Let each team up with the other.

Just as you may sometimes outrace yourself and find it wise to restrain your reading pace, so will you occasionally find that you are remembering less, or that things you think you should have remembered have begun to slip from mind. This may be due to more extensive reading than formerly, with too many new facts crowding out the old. But more likely, the memory of the old is simply dormant.

Always, you can go back and read over old material as a "refresher" and this is where you can turn to appropriate methods given in this book. In the old days, people favored reading the same thing over and over in grim, slavish fashion, feeling that it would have to be learned by rote in order to stick. But that is not so.

In reviving dormant memory, you can often skim and scan, instead of reading closely. You can touch up the parts that you missed, or where you find yourself weak, by utilizing one of the general reading techniques that we have described. Finally, if a few needed points still won't stay in mind, or prove harder to peg, you can set them more firmly through an artificial memory device, properly employed.

Applying Methods of Analysis to Reading and Reading Ability

All these factors work in future reading as well as with past. The more you know about your reading, and the more you familiarize yourself with all the ways to read faster and remember more, the better you can analyze both your reading and your reading problems as you proceed.

In certain reading, you will see a similarity in style with something you have read before. During other reading, you will realize that certain facts should be pegged early, while in other cases, they can wait. You will recognize when you can and should use some of the general reading techniques and memory aids that are at your disposal.

For certain types of reading, this analytical ability is more than half the battle and it can be built by using it constantly, together with applying your handy methods whenever your analysis calls for them. You will find, too, that in analyzing reading, you tend to go further and analyze the content of the material itself. All this comes through reading to remember.

Good reading methods mean good reading, and good reading should improve your personality. It gives you more to think about, widens your range of knowledge, and enables you to analyze people better, as well as the things that you have read. Often, you can compare your own reactions with those of other persons, when discussing books or subjects which you have both read. The more attention you have given to the systematic mastery of reading and remembering, the better your results will be in comparison.

What You Gain Through Reading and Remembering; How to Use This Skill

The main reason is that through gearing reading with remembering, you acquire deeper knowledge, rather than casual knowledge. You are always noting how you can improve your methods, and by doing so, you will improve them. On the other hand, careless readers are satisfied with superficiality and often dismiss as trivial the things they cannot remember. Even as you acquire this new agility at reading to remember, you should also study the way to use it.

Avoid flashing your ability. Don't talk about your reading speed or how much you remember. Just keep up a proper pace, watching your own improvement, and keeping all comparisons to yourself. Use tact in social circles; don't correct other people and tell them that they are wrong about something they read, unless it is an extreme case. If there are doubts, let them ask you.

In final counsel, through reading and remembering, try to build a solid structure, brick by brick. That simile is a good one, for reading is like a steady prolonged building process that is judged only as it begins to gain monumental proportions, or approaches a state of completion. As you learn to read faster and remember more, your new ability to appraise your own work will enable you to look back in an enlightened way upon the things accomplished. At the same time, you will become more able to set your eye on a creative future, with the present the guide by which you can pave the way.

Index

A

Acronyms, memory device, 128-129, 173, 228
Acrostics, 130-131, 173-174, 228
  variations, 133-135
Addresses, remembering, 168
Alphabet, value of learning, 3, 57
Art, reading skill as, 207, 223-224
Association, 117
  factors aiding, 64, 128, 225
  key to memorizing, 8-9, 89-90
  pronunciation and, 59-60
  visualization used to stimulate, 10, 67-68
Attention, maintaining, 2, 5-8, 90, 117, 225
Author's style, familiarity with, 98-99, 214

B

"Back sweep," 37-39, 41, 216, 220
Bacon, Roger, 140, 167-168
Barnum, P.T., 156-157
Basic reading mechanics, 31-52, 54-55
Benchley, Robert, 4
Book, position while reading, 23
Book condensations, 121, 215

C

Carnegie, Dale, 120-121
"Catch-and-carry-over" glimpses, 70
Categories (word game), 180-183
Chain system, 127, 147-151, 228
  Figure Alphabet used with, 167-168

procedure, 147-150
summary, 150-151
Check-backs, 83, 85, 207
  on difficult words, 214
  value of, 210
Cicero, 139, 142
Columbus, Christopher, 164-165
Column width, 41, 216-218
Comprehension, 6, 14
  breaking the "barrier," 55-56
  effect of typography, 218-223
  extending, 53
  problem of "fogging," 212-216
  pronunciation and, 59-60
  ratio of retention and, 208-209
  reading faster and, 207-210
  use of vocalization, 56-59
Concentration, 17, 28
Conditions for reading, 15-30, 225-226
  avoiding poor, 18-19
  while traveling, 19-20
Cross motion, 216
Crossword puzzles, 173, 174-175
Cryptograms, 175-176
Cultural reading, 108-112
  philosophical works, 110-111
  reviewing and checking points, 110
  rules, 110, 111-112

D

Dates, remembering, 229
  Figure Alphabet system, 153, 164-167
Davis, Richard Harding, 100-104
Daylight reading, 19, 21-22

233

T

U

V